MATTHEW

REFORMED EXPOSITORY BIBLE STUDIES

A Companion Series to the Reformed Expository Commentaries

Series Editors

Daniel M. Doriani
Iain M. Duguid
Richard D. Phillips
Philip Graham Ryken

Esther & Ruth: The Lord Delivers and Redeems
Daniel: Faith Enduring through Adversity
Matthew: Making Disciples for the Nations (two volumes)
Galatians: The Gospel of Free Grace
Hebrews: Standing Firm in Christ
James: Portrait of a Living Faith

MATTHEW

MAKING DISCIPLES FOR THE NATIONS
Volume 1 (Chapters 1–13)

A 13-LESSON STUDY

REFORMED EXPOSITORY
BIBLE STUDY

JON NIELSON
and DANIEL M. DORIANI

PUBLISHING
P.O. BOX 817 • PHILLIPSBURG • NEW JERSEY 08865-0817

ISBN: 978-1-62995-761-6 (pbk)
ISBN: 978-1-62995-762-3 (ePub)
ISBN: 978-1-62995-763-0 (Mobi)

CONTENTS

SERIES INTRODUCTION

Studying the Bible will change your life. This is the consistent witness of Scripture and the experience of people all over the world, in every period of church history.

King David said, "The law of the LORD is perfect, reviving the soul; the testimony of the LORD is sure, making wise the simple; the precepts of the LORD are right, rejoicing the heart; the commandment of the LORD is pure, enlightening the eyes" (Ps. 19:7–8). So anyone who wants to be wiser and happier, and who wants to feel more alive, with a clearer perception of spiritual reality, should study the Scriptures.

Whether we study the Bible alone or with other Christians, it will change us from the inside out. The Reformed Expository Bible Studies provide tools for biblical transformation. Written as a companion to the Reformed Expository Commentary, this series of short books for personal or group study is designed to help people study the Bible for themselves, understand its message, and then apply its truths to daily life.

Each Bible study is introduced by a pastor-scholar who has written a full-length expository commentary on the same book of the Bible. The individual chapters start with the summary of a Bible passage, explaining **The Big Picture** of this portion of God's Word. Then the questions in **Getting Started** introduce one or two of the passage's main themes in ways that connect to life experience. These questions may be especially helpful for group leaders in generating lively conversation.

Understanding the Bible's message starts with seeing what is actually there, which is where **Observing the Text** comes in. Then the Bible study provides a longer and more in-depth set of questions entitled **Understanding the Text**. These questions carefully guide students through the entire passage, verse by verse or section by section.

It is important not to read a Bible passage in isolation, but to see it in the wider context of Scripture. So each Bible study includes two **Bible Connections** questions that invite readers to investigate passages from other places in Scripture—passages that add important background, offer valuable contrasts or comparisons, and especially connect the main passage to the person and work of Jesus Christ.

The next section is one of the most distinctive features of the Reformed Expository Bible Studies. The authors believe that the Bible teaches important doctrines of the Christian faith, and that reading biblical literature is enhanced when we know something about its underlying theology. The questions in **Theology Connections** identify some of these doctrines by bringing the Bible passage into conversation with creeds and confessions from the Reformed tradition, as well as with learned theologians of the church.

Our aim in all of this is to help ordinary Christians apply biblical truth to daily life. **Applying the Text** uses open-ended questions to get people thinking about sins that need to be confessed, attitudes that need to change, and areas of new obedience that need to come alive by the power and influence of the Holy Spirit. Finally, each study ends with a **Prayer Prompt** that invites Bible students to respond to what they are learning with petitions for God's help and words of praise and gratitude.

You will notice boxed quotations throughout the Bible study. These quotations come from one of the volumes in the Reformed Expository Commentary. Although the Bible study can stand alone and includes everything you need for a life-changing encounter with a book of the Bible, it is also intended to serve as a companion to a full commentary on the same biblical book. Reading the full commentary is especially useful for teachers who want to help their students answer the questions in the Bible study at a deeper level, as well as for students who wish to further enrich their own biblical understanding.

The people who worked together to produce this series of Bible studies have prayed that they will engage you more intimately with Scripture, producing the kind of spiritual transformation that only the Bible can bring.

Philip Graham Ryken
Coeditor of the Reformed Expository Commentary series

INTRODUCING MATTHEW

The four gospels are equally inspired and equally essential for the church. Yet Matthew can be described as the first gospel of the church. For centuries, church leaders believed it to be the first that was written. It also contains the greatest portion of teaching on the Christian life out of any of the gospels and offers the most guidance regarding the use of the Old Testament. It became the best known and most used gospel. Once that happened, scholars note, its status became self-perpetuating.

We often study Matthew a verse or chapter at a time—but Matthew is a complete historical narrative that has a grand purpose. Like the other gospels, Matthew is both a factual account of Jesus's life and a faith-inviting testimony to the person and work of Jesus. The authors of all four gospels marshaled evidence that Jesus is Son of God and Savior in order that people might believe in him, receive his salvation, and follow him.

In its early chapters, Matthew establishes Jesus's identity: He is Jesus—which means "God saves"—for he will save his people from their sins (1:1, 21). He is the Christ—the one who was anointed by God for a given task (1:1, 18). He is the son of David—the king of the Jews (1:1; 2:2). He is the son of Abraham; he will bring blessing to the nations (1:1, 17; see also Gen. 12:2–3). He is born of a virgin—born of the Holy Spirit (1:18–20). He is Immanuel—God with us (1:23). He is the king of the Jews (2:2), the sinless son of Adam, and the heir of Israel[1] (4:1–11). Eventually, the disciples know that he is "the Christ, the Son of living God" (16:16).

Most Jewish leaders, motivated in part by envy (27:18), thought that

---

1. For more on Jesus as the new Adam and the one true Israelite, see the accompanying Reformed Expository Commentary: Daniel M. Doriani, *Matthew*, vol. 1, *Chapters 1–13* (Phillipsburg, NJ: P&R Publishing, 2008), 76–80.

he was dangerous—a lawbreaker who deluded the people—but both the crowds and the disciples accepted Jesus as a prophet, teacher, and healer. Yet he insisted that he is more: the Suffering Servant, the Son of Man who "came not to be served but to serve, and to give his life as a ransom for many" (20:28; see also vv. 26–27). Thus Jesus foretold his substitutionary death repeatedly (16:21; 17:22–23; 20:17–19), even if the disciples understood and believed only after his resurrection.

After the reader meets him in chapters 1–4 of Matthew, Jesus establishes in chapters 5–7 what it means to be a disciple. He then, in chapters 8–9, verifies the authority of his words through authoritative deeds—his miraculous healings. In chapter 10, after he calls the twelve disciples (or apostles), he sends them out to proclaim the kingdom. The response, as we see in chapters 11–12, is mixed; and Jesus explains in chapter 13 that the kingdom comes in a weak and hidden form, like seed scattered—not like armies marching. After a season when he is largely alone and is training the disciples, in chapters 14–18, Jesus returns to the public eye in chapters 19–20 and, in chapter 21, enters Jerusalem, where he judges the temple. After several days when he teaches in public and in private, in chapters 22–25, the leaders of Israel in chapters 26–27 make use of Judas's betrayal to arrest, torment, try, and finally kill Jesus, with the cowardly complicity of Rome. This is history's greatest tragedy and greatest injustice—yet it became God's greatest victory when Jesus rose from death, in the flesh, on Easter morning, as we see in chapter 28. By his suffering he bore our sins, and by his life we live.

In contrast to the New Testament epistles, no gospel names its **author**. Still, from the first, the church universally testified that Matthew—one of the twelve, an eye- and earwitness of Jesus's ministry, and a tax collector—wrote the first gospel. Its order and precision fit the idea that it was written by a man who kept orderly records. It is difficult to date Matthew, but evangelical scholars agree that chapter 24 of the book describes the fall of Jerusalem as a future event, meaning that Matthew had to be written before A.D. 70.

The question of the book's **audience** is weightier than that of its date. While the gospels tell a single story, they differ regarding many of the details they highlight and the secondary goals that each one presents, and these differences offer hints about each author's purpose. There is a consensus that in some sense Matthew wrote for Jews. Clearly the readers who would most easily understand Matthew are Jewish readers. Of the four gospels, Matthew makes the most references to Jewish customs and regulations, touching on Sabbath regulations, divorce, ceremonial washing, fasting, taxes, phylacteries, tombs, and more. He also quotes the Old Testament six times in the first few chapters, to induce readers to see Jesus's life in terms of Israel's history and prophecies. Matthew even phrases Jesus's language for Jewish readers. For example, he generally says "kingdom of heaven" instead of "kingdom of God," since observant Jews tried to avoid using God's name. Matthew also presents Jesus's life in ways that would appeal to Israelites. So Jesus is the Messiah, and his genealogy goes back to Abraham, the father of the Jews, and to David, the king of the Jews. The account of magi coming to worship Jesus fulfills Jewish expectations that the nations would come to Jerusalem. And Jesus often speaks of the law, rightly interpreted, as a means of promoting righteousness (Matt. 5–6, 23)—something that surely appealed to Jews.

Yet Matthew has great interest in Gentiles too. While his genealogy of Jesus (1:1–17) traces back to Abraham, the father of the Jews, it also mentions Gentile women: Rahab and Ruth (v. 5). In the birth narratives that he presents, only Gentiles worship Jesus; while Herod, the scribes, and the people of Jerusalem are hostile or indifferent (2:1–15). Jesus's ministry begins in "Galilee of the Gentiles" (4:15), and he heals people from the Gentile lands (4:17–25). Even within Israel's borders, an early miracle of Jesus benefits a Gentile—a centurion—whom he praises for showing faith that exceeds that which he has found in Israel (8:5–13). Jesus focuses on the lost sheep of Israel (10:5–6), but he also ministers to Gentiles whom he meets (15:21–28).

So it is best to say that Matthew wrote to move Jews to believe that Jesus is the Messiah and to equip believing Jews to take the message of Jesus, the Savior and Lord, to the Gentiles. In his call for Israel to believe, Jesus also warned them of the consequences of unbelief. If they rejected his message, they would be "thrown into the outer darkness" (8:12). If they failed to bear fruit for God, Jesus told them that "the kingdom of God will be taken away from you and given to a people producing its fruits" (21:43). So the gospel of Matthew urges Israel to receive its Messiah, to bear appropriate fruit, and to share its faith with the nations.

Matthew states his great **purpose** as he concludes. When Jesus commissioned the disciples to "make disciples of all nations" and to "observe all that [he had] commanded" (28:19–20), he was speaking both to them and to all church generations that were to follow (2 Tim. 2:2). Of the four gospels, Matthew dedicates the most of its space to Jesus's teaching. That teaching addresses most of the issues that faced his disciples in that age and would go on to face them in every age.

All gospels present two truths: it is hard to be a disciple, and yet anyone can be a disciple. Matthew encourages his reader to identify with the Twelve as they grow in discipleship. Throughout his gospel, he shows Jesus describing the Twelve with the distinct term *oligopistos*, which means "of little faith" (Matt. 6:30; 8:26; 14:31; 16:8—see also Luke 12:28).This suggests that they have *some* faith. They may be weak, they may err, but they also grow until the end and become apostles—ones who are ready to hear and implement the Great Commission. When Jesus describes them this way, we read it as a direct address: "*you* of little faith." Thus Jesus wants *us* to share the experience of the first apostles. *We* should grow from having a little faith to having a strong faith, so that we can make disciples in our generation among both Jews and Gentiles and inspire other generations to come.

Matthew's orderly mind and zeal for Jesus's teachings give his gospel a unique double **structure**. It describes Jesus's life in a series of narrative phases and also intersperses five key discourses throughout the action.

> The Origin, Birth, and Identity of Jesus (1:1–2:23)
> The Preparation and Early Ministry in Galilee (3:1–4:25)
> *The First Discourse: Discipleship in Jesus's Kingdom (5:1–7:29)*
> The Kingdom's Growth under Jesus's Authority (8:1–10:42)
> > *The Second Discourse: The Disciples Follow Jesus into Mission (10:1–11:1)*
> The Kingdom's Growth in the Face of Resistance (11:2–13:58)
> > *The Third Discourse: Parables of the Kingdom (13:1–52)*
> Training the Disciples among Crowds and Leaders (14:1–20:34)
> > *The Fourth Discourse: Community Life in the Kingdom (18:1–35)*
> Conflict and Teaching in Jerusalem (21:1–23:39)

The Fifth Discourse: Trouble, Perseverance, and the Eschaton (24:1–25:46)
Death, and Resurrection (26:1–28:20)

Each discourse begins by mentioning an audience for Jesus's teaching. Each ends with a variation of the phrase "when Jesus had finished saying these things . . ." And each block of teaching fits perfectly within the rest of the gospel story. As crowds flock to Jesus in Matthew 4, he offers the Sermon on the Mount (First Discourse), which describes the thoughts and deeds of a disciple. After he ministers widely and calls the Twelve to join him, he describes their mission and the mindset they must bring to it (Second Discourse). When Jewish society largely rejects Jesus, he explains how his kingdom comes (Third Discourse). After he instructs the disciples, he teaches them how to live in community (Fourth Discourse). As he prepares to die, he describes the future of Israel, the disciples, and mankind (Fifth Discourse).Thus Jesus delivers five discourses, which echo the five books of Moses and guide his disciples who live in Israel, throughout the empire, and beyond—which includes us in the present day. So Matthew both wrote and organized his gospel in order that we may believe, become disciples, and make disciples in turn.

Daniel M. Doriani
Coeditor of the Reformed Expository Commentary series
Coeditor of the Reformed Expository Bible Study series
Author of *Matthew* (REC)

LESSON 1

THE ENTRANCE OF THE KING

Matthew 1:1–2:23

THE BIG PICTURE

In the opening two chapters of his gospel, Matthew introduces us, in his own particular fashion, to Jesus Christ. While Luke's gospel begins with an introduction, John's with a theological explanation, and Mark's with a breathless rush to begin the story, Matthew chooses to begin with a genealogy, as he traces the human lineage of Jesus all the way back to Abraham. Far from merely being a literary convention, this genealogy serves to establish the royal line of the one who truly comes as the Christ, the Messiah, the son of David—the king of the Jews. The opening titles that Matthew gives to Jesus—"Christ"; "son of David"; "son of Abraham"—have massive biblical significance; they point to Jesus as being the Anointed One, the promised ruler, and the blessed descendant of the Jewish patriarchs. His reign will not be a purely political one, however—Matthew's intentional inclusion of Gentile women (Tamar, Rahab, Ruth) in this genealogy points us to the global salvation that King Jesus will bring.

Matthew follows his genealogy with the well-known record of the birth of Jesus Christ—although the only angelic visit he includes is the one that is made to Joseph, when he is assured that he should take Mary as his wife. Matthew's focus turns quickly to the visit of the "wise men from the east," who come to Jerusalem following a star and seeking to worship the King of the Jews (2:1; see also vv. 2–12). Their worship of another "king" pushes King Herod into a murderous rage, as he commands that all male children in the region surrounding Bethlehem be put to death. Joseph and Mary protect Jesus by sojourning in Egypt until the death of Herod, after which they return and settle in the city of Nazareth. Here, in this small town, the true King and Messiah will be raised—the son of a humble carpenter, and yet the one who will bring God's saving promises to his people.

Read Matthew 1:1–2:23.

GETTING STARTED

1. Why is understanding someone's "backstory" so important? How do a person's history, background, and beginnings enable you to better grasp that person's identity?

2. What would you consider to be the most well-known details and aspects of the story of Jesus's birth? Why might not all of the gospel writers have included the same parts of the story?

The Hero of Matthew's Gospel, pg. 5

Matthew tells us who Jesus is. Yet his nature is never separated from his work, for he is the Savior for the nations. Matthew 1:1 introduces us to the hero by stating his name and his origin. He is Jesus the Savior, Christ the anointed, the son of Abraham, hence of both pagan and Jewish lineage, and he is the Son of David, the great king.

OBSERVING THE TEXT

3. Don't merely rush through the genealogy that begins the gospel of Matthew; read it carefully. What do you notice about the people who are included? What women are included, and what is said about them?

4. Consider the actions and obedience that Joseph and Mary display throughout these opening chapters. What does God reveal to them, and how does he give them this revelation? What are they told about the child who will be born to them?

5. How does King Herod react to the news of another "king of the Jews"? In what ways does God sovereignly work to protect Jesus? How is Matthew showing his readers the identity of Jesus, even in these opening chapters?

UNDERSTANDING THE TEXT

6. How do the opening titles that Matthew gives to Jesus begin to teach us about his identity (1:1)? Why are these such important titles, with regard to Old Testament history and the expectations of God's Old Testament people?

7. Why might Matthew have chosen to tell the birth story of Jesus by focusing largely on Joseph's experience (1:18–25)? How does the angel identify Joseph, and why is that significant to an understanding of Jesus's human origin (1:20)? What does the angel explain to Joseph about the Holy Spirit, in that same verse, and why is that significant to an understanding of Jesus's divine origin as well?

The Promise of Something Different, pg. 15

Matthew reveals that Jesus is from the *line* of David, but not from the *flesh* of David. The promises to David's line showed that Israel needed a mighty deliverer, a great and fearless king, a warrior to battle foes, and a man who loved God and his people more than life itself. Yet . . . human flesh could not deliver God's people. They needed something different.

8. What is the significance of the name "Immanuel," which Matthew attaches to Jesus after recording the angel's words? From where does the prophecy in verse 23 come? What was its original context, and how is Matthew now applying it to Jesus and his birth?

9. How does Matthew intentionally contrast the earnest seeking of the wise men with the murderous envy of King Herod throughout the opening verses of Matthew 2 (vv. 1–12)? What role do the "chief priests and scribes" play in the story, and how would you describe their response to the birth of Jesus (2:4–6)? What is the wise men's response to seeing Jesus (2:10–11)?

10. What Old Testament prophecy does Matthew intentionally connect to Joseph, Mary, and Jesus's flight to Egypt (2:15)? What does this suggest about Matthew's audience—and about what he expects them to know and value?

11. How does Herod's murderous rage echo the actions of Pharaoh from the opening chapter of Exodus? What do we learn from King Herod about the response of a sinful world to the coming of the Son of God?

BIBLE CONNECTIONS

12. Matthew quotes from Isaiah 7 when the angel appears to Joseph. Now read Isaiah 9:6–7, which is further Old Testament prophecy about the coming "child" from God. What promises are attached to the coming of this Son of God? How is it evident that Isaiah looks forward to someone who is far greater than any merely human king?

13. Read Revelation 12:1–6. How does this passage describe Satan's ongoing war against God's Son and God's people? In what ways do these early years of Jesus Christ shine a light on the rage, hatred, and murderous malice of the enemies of God?

THEOLOGY CONNECTIONS

14. In 451, the Council of Chalcedon was convened, with the purpose of clarifying Jesus Christ's unified nature as the God-man. Central to its purpose was clearly articulating the biblical and orthodox truth that Jesus is, and was, fully God and fully human—without confusion, division, separation, or change. How is this doctrine explained to us, at least in part, through the account of the visit of the angel of the Lord to Joseph? Why is this doctrine so crucial to the Christian faith?

15. The Westminster Larger Catechism, in answer 37, describes the incarnation of Jesus in this way: "Christ the Son of God became man, by taking to himself a true body, and a reasonable soul, being conceived by the power of the Holy Ghost in the womb of the Virgin Mary, of her substance, and born of her, yet without sin." What are the important distinctions and clarifications that this explanation makes? How are some of them demonstrated in the narrative account of Matthew 1?

APPLYING THE TEXT

16. What assurance and hope should the genealogy of Jesus Christ give to sinners who need grace? How can its mention of sinful kings and female Gentile "outsiders" remind you of your gracious Savior who came to call sinners from all nations?

17. What can Matthew's titles for Jesus, as well as his repeated mentions of Old Testament prophecies that were fulfilled through Jesus's coming, teach you about the unity of God's work throughout history? How should the fact that God keeps his promises and fulfills his covenant encourage you in your walk with him today?

18. How ought the murderous violence that was directed toward Jesus, even from his earliest days, shape our understanding of sin, evil, and Satan? How should we make sense of the ongoing conflict in our world, even as we trust that Jesus Christ will have the ultimate victory over Satan?

PRAYER PROMPT

While you certainly cannot plumb the depths of the mysteries of the virgin birth, the incarnation, and the Satanic opposition to and prophetic fulfillment of the coming of Jesus Christ, your study of these first two chapters of the gospel of Matthew should give you a richer understanding of these cosmic events. Today, as you close your study with prayer, praise God for fulfilling his promises, as well as the expectations that his people held for centuries, by sending his Son to be the great son of David, son of Abraham, Christ, and "Immanuel"—God with us. Thank him for preserving Jesus from early assaults on his life, as well as preserving the church of Jesus amidst the constant Satanic assaults of those who oppose his rule to this day. And ask him for strength, and for faith in his Son, as you live for him in the week ahead.

A Peek behind the Curtain, pg. 46

Matthew 2 shows us what Herod tried to do to the Christ child and how he and his parents escaped. Revelation 12 lets us peek behind the curtain and see the author of history at work. . . . A dragon crouches to devour the child at the moment of his birth. He snaps but misses, for God will preserve him. The Lord is master of history. He will save his people through this child.

LESSON 2

PREPARING AND BEGINNING

Matthew 3:1-4:25

THE BIG PICTURE

Matthew 3 begins by turning our attention to John the Baptist's prophetic announcement of the coming ministry of Jesus (3:1–12). Matthew intentionally links John to the Old Testament promises regarding a prophetic forerunner to the Messiah—a forerunner who calls out from the wilderness for the people of God to repent and prepare themselves. John rails against religious hypocrisy and points to the powerful coming of Jesus, who will baptize people with the very "Holy Spirit and fire" of God (3:11). Jesus himself then enters onto the scene for the first time as an adult, as he is baptized by John in the Jordan River and receives words of commendation from God the Father and God the Holy Spirit (3:13–17). But he is then quickly driven into the wilderness, where he faces a direct onslaught of temptation from the devil, and he overcomes this attack by holding fast to the Word of God at every test (4:1–11). Jesus then moves to Capernaum, where his public ministry begins; there he gathers disciples to himself and ministers to great crowds of people (4:12–25).

Throughout this entire section, Matthew is intent on showing his readers the fulfillment of Old Testament prophecy as Jesus breaks onto the stage of his gospel with the dawning of his public ministry. Jesus comes with prophetic announcement, receives the commendation of God himself, and walks in perfect obedience to God's Word; he passes every test that Israel has failed and begins to proclaim God's joyful news of salvation (4:17). He passes through the waters of baptism, which calls our minds back to the Red Sea crossing. He overcomes temptation in the wilderness—unlike the Israelites, who succumbed to sin again and again during their wilderness wanderings. Jesus then begins to gather a people to himself—they will be the new "Israel" of God, and he will be their great Teacher, Healer, Prophet, and King.

Read Matthew 3:1–4:25.

GETTING STARTED

1. What are some ways in which people tend to act sorry for wrong things they have done while falling short of displaying true repentance for sin? How can you identify true repentance? What are the marks of genuine sorrow for sin and of a changed heart?

2. How did the Israelites demonstrate their failure in obedience, faith, and worship throughout the Old Testament? Why is it so important for us to understand the perfect obedient *life* that Jesus lived, as well as the *death* that he died on the cross?

Only a Voice, pg. 56
Although John was the greatest man of his generation, acclaimed in all the land, Jesus is far greater. . . . John says he is not worthy to be Jesus' slave. As he says this, he tells his listeners to look to Jesus, not to him. Every church must repeat this testimony. The greatest prophet is only a voice, but Jesus is the Redeemer.

OBSERVING THE TEXT

3. What does Matthew seem to emphasize most about John the Baptist (3:1–12)? What is important about his appearance and location? What are the key points of his message? How does he prepare the people effectively for the coming of Jesus?

4. Consider the baptism and temptation of Jesus. How might these events intentionally echo the experience of the Israelites in the Old Testament? Why might this be important?

5. How does Matthew demonstrate the holiness and perfect obedience of Jesus throughout this passage? What seems to be the main purpose of Jesus's ministry as he begins to preach publicly?

UNDERSTANDING THE TEXT

6. What does the baptism of John the Baptist symbolize (3:6, 11)? How does John contrast his ministry with the ministry of Jesus—the one

who will follow him (3:11–12)? What aspects of Jesus's work and call does he emphasize as he prepares the people for his coming?

7. Why might John have initially sought to prevent Jesus from being baptized by him (3:14)? How does Jesus's answer explain his purpose for being baptized? What do the voice from heaven and the descent of the Spirit of God say about the identity of Jesus (3:16–17)?

8. How would you describe the essence, or substance, of the different temptations that the devil puts before Jesus in the wilderness (4:3, 6, 9)? In what way are those temptations part of a dangerous and powerful strategy?

Unique and Beloved, pg. 62

When John baptized Jesus, a voice also came from heaven, saying, "This is my Son, whom I love; with him I am well pleased" (3:17). . . . Matthew has already said he is the Son of David and the son of Abraham (1:1). He was conceived by the Holy Spirit. He is Immanuel and he will save his people from their sins (1:20–23). Now we also know he is the unique and beloved Son of God.

9. What does Jesus do in response to the temptation of the devil, and why is this such an important model for us (4:4, 7, 10)? How does Jesus's resistance to the devil contrast with the behavior of the Israelites in the wilderness following their deliverance from Egypt?

10. As Jesus begins his ministry, Matthew summarizes the message of his preaching with these words: "Repent, for the kingdom of heaven is at hand" (4:17). How should we understand the phrase "the kingdom of heaven"? In what ways has the coming of Jesus to earth inaugurated the kingdom? How has the kingdom still not fully arrived?

11. What do you notice about Jesus's gathering of the first disciples? What kind of men are they, and how do they respond to Jesus (4:22)? What is the general response to the beginning of Jesus's public ministry (4:23–25)?

BIBLE CONNECTIONS

12. The New Testament certainly did not introduce the concept of repentance. Read Isaiah 55:7. How is repentance defined in this

Old-Testament passage? What is promised to those who truly repent and turn to God in faith?

13. Read Genesis 3:1–6—a passage that records for us another direct onslaught of temptation from Satan against humanity. What strategy does Satan take with Eve, and how does he succeed? What is different about the way that Jesus resists him? In what way does this show us the purpose behind Jesus's coming as a human man, as well as what he accomplished?

THEOLOGY CONNECTIONS

14. In preparation for the coming of Jesus, John the Baptist delivers a message of repentance, and baptism is the accompanying sign of this repentant spirit (Matt. 3:2, 8). The Westminster Larger Catechism defines repentance in this way in answer 76: "Repentance unto life is a saving grace, wrought in the heart of a sinner by the Spirit and word of God, whereby . . . he so grieves for and hates his sins, as that he turns from them all to God, purposing and endeavoring constantly to walk with him in all the ways of new obedience." How is this definition of repentance helpful? In what ways does it explain what John the Baptist desired from his audience in the wilderness?

15. The death and suffering of Jesus on the cross are often referred to as the "passive" obedience of Jesus—he submitted to the punishment of sin in the place of God's sinful people. The "active" obedience of Jesus, then, refers to his perfect fulfillment of the law of God in every way. How does Matthew 4:1–11 give us a picture of Jesus's "active" obedience to God and his Word, even in the midst of a direct attack from Satan?

APPLYING THE TEXT

16. How can you be sure that you have truly repented of your sins? What can ongoing repentance look like—and what *should* it look like—in the life of a Christian?

17. Why is it so important for us to understand that Jesus succeeded where all of God's people had failed, in the areas of resisting temptation, obeying God's Word, and rejecting sin? How do you need to grow in your understanding that Jesus is your substitute, advocate, and representative before God?

18. What can you learn from Jesus about the way that you ought to battle and resist temptation? How could God's Word play a larger role in your resistance to sin and disobedience?

PRAYER PROMPT

As you conclude your study of this passage today, consider the glorious reality of the coming of Jesus Christ to our world. He is the answer to the prophetic hopes and longings of God's people; he comes with perfect obedience and with the public approval of God the Father and God the Holy Spirit. Best of all, Jesus comes to inaugurate a kingdom that will be wide open to all who humbly repent and put their faith in him! Today, thank God for throwing wide the entrance of the kingdom of heaven to you, as he did for his very disciples, through the coming of his Son Jesus. Pray that he would give you a deeper appreciation of *your* inclusion in his glorious heavenly kingdom.

The Fullness of the Kingdom, pgs. 90–91

The kingdom has arrived, and, subversively enough, sinners, prodigals, and other underachievers are in, while the religious elite are out. But even while Jesus' disciples take the kingdom as a present possession, the fullness of the kingdom lies ahead, so that Jesus can tell us to pray that his kingdom come (Matt. 6:10). The kingdom is growing toward a great climax, when God will root out every cause of sin, when people from every nation will stream into the kingdom.

LESSON 3

JESUS THE PREACHER

Matthew 5:1–26

THE BIG PICTURE

As Matthew 4 concluded, we saw the launch of Jesus's public ministry and the beginning of his role as a preacher of the kingdom of God. Now, in Matthew 5, we come to Jesus's longest recorded sermon, which spans chapters 5 through 7. Often called the "Sermon on the Mount," this collection of teachings is essentially an explication of God's law—one that applies it to Jesus's disciples as they come to him and learn to follow him (5:1). Jesus begins by declaring a word of "blessing" from God on those who demonstrate the kind of character that reflects the values of the kingdom of God (5:2–11). He calls his disciples to shine brightly in the world as they live out their calling (5:13–16). He is careful to clarify that his teaching is not a rejection of the law of God; rather, he teaches authoritatively about the true fulfillment of the law of God, which can come only through following him (5:17–20). In this way, the disciples of Jesus can actually surpass the merely outward "righteousness" of the Jewish religious leaders (5:20). Finally, Jesus begins to focus on particular Old Testament commands, beginning with "You shall not murder" (5:21–26). He demonstrates the true meaning of this command—as well as its prohibition not only against killing someone but even against hating another person in one's heart. Jesus is interpreting and applying the law of God from a place of authority, showing how God's character must be reflected in the lives of those who follow him as true disciples.

Read Matthew 5:1–26.

GETTING STARTED

1. What would you identify as some of the explicit or implicit core values of the culture in which you live? What do people value as matters of ultimate importance? How do some of these values contrast with the values of God and his gospel?

2. What are some ways in which people seek to appear good, kind, or respectable in the eyes of others? What kinds of sinful attitudes can people keep hidden and secret without damaging their public reputation?

A Call for Disciples, pg. 106

Miracles made Jesus popular. But Jesus wanted *disciples*, not *crowds*, so he called a few men to himself. To do so, he separated them from the crowds, for the crowds did not necessarily follow him for the best reasons. . . . Jesus never intended to heal all the sick in Israel. He sought to raise up true disciples. So Jesus called his disciples to himself, sat down, and began to teach them.

OBSERVING THE TEXT

3. How would you describe the general pattern of Jesus's repeated phrases throughout Matthew 5:2–11? What might he be communicating through this use of repetition and this style of speech?

4. Consider the metaphors that Jesus uses to describe his disciples (5:13–16) as well as the other ways that he describes them throughout this passage. What kind of a picture is he painting of his followers—and how does this picture show that they are to be distinct and different from the world?

5. How does it become apparent toward the end of this passage that Jesus is calling his disciples to go beyond surface-level obedience to the law and to be transformed inwardly as well as externally (5:17–26)?

UNDERSTANDING THE TEXT

6. What does a careful reading of Matthew 5:1 tell you about the intended audience of Jesus's extended sermon in these chapters? Why is it so significant to understand this point?

7. As you read carefully through the "Beatitudes" of Matthew 5:2–11, which would you identify as being particularly countercultural, with regard to the common values and practices of the world? How is Jesus demonstrating the upside-down nature of the kingdom of God compared to the kingdom of the world?

8. What are some of the promises that are attached to the "blessed" attitudes and actions that Jesus identifies (5:2–11)? Where, and how, ought followers of Jesus to expect to receive their reward for obedience to his Word?

9. What are the main metaphors that Jesus uses for God's people in Matthew 5:13–16—and how ought those metaphors to shape our understanding of our role in the world?

Act Like What You Are, pg. 137

So then, there are four possible responses to a disciple's faithful life. At the extremes are persecution and praise of God. Between them, we can serve as salt and light. Jesus says we *are* different, and therefore we are accountable to act like it. Let us accept the responsibility to *be* the light of the world. Let us not fail due to laziness, compromise, or fear. Let us act boldly and speak freely, leaving the results to God.

10. How does Jesus carefully explain the way that his teaching relates to the law of Moses (5:17–20)? How do his words in this section refute any critique that he is relaxing, or negating, the law of God?

11. How does Jesus explain and expand the Old Testament command against murder (5:21–26)? What is he teaching about the secret sinfulness of the human heart?

BIBLE CONNECTIONS

12. Read Exodus 19:16–20. How would you describe the picture of the mountain, as God prepares to give his Word to his people through Moses? What is similar about the scene in Matthew 5–7? What is different?

13. Read 1 Peter 2:19–23. How does the apostle Peter further develop the theme of persecution "for righteousness' sake" that we see in Matthew 5:10, which Jesus declares to be "blessed"?

THEOLOGY CONNECTIONS

14. The Westminster Confession of Faith declares this about the moral law of God: "The moral law doth forever bind all, as well justified persons as others, to the obedience thereof; and that not only in regard of the matter contained in it, but also in respect of the authority of God the Creator, who gave it. Neither doth Christ, in the Gospel, any way dissolve . . . this obligation" (19.5). How is this statement in agreement with the words of Jesus you have just studied in this passage?

15. Answer 105 of the Heidelberg Catechism asserts that the sixth commandment tells us "that I, neither in thought, nor in word or gesture, much less in deed, [am to] dishonor, hate, wound, or kill my neighbor." How is this catechism answer seeking to apply the teaching of Jesus to this commandment against murder?

APPLYING THE TEXT

16. How do your ways of speaking, thinking, or acting need to be continually reordered by the "beatitudes" of Jesus (5:2–11)? In what ways has the world shaped your view of what is "blessed" more than the Word of God has?

17. Why do you sometimes fail to remember that your role is to be "salt" and "light" in the world, through your witness to Jesus? How can you more actively and intentionally remember this calling?

18. Based on Jesus's teaching about murder (as well as anger and hatred), whom do you need to forgive? With whom do you need to reconcile? Why is it so dangerous for us to harbor hatred—even secretly and internally?

Being Peaceful; Making Peace, pg. 148

The command "Do not murder" seems so simple. It is familiar, it protects us, and, externally at least, it is easy to observe. But Jesus comes to fulfill the law, to disclose its complete meaning, which is this: We must give up rage and contempt. We must be peaceful and make peace, with both brothers and enemies, with those whom we offend and with those who wrongly take offense.

PRAYER PROMPT

As you have seen in your study of the first half of Matthew 5, Jesus's teaching calls his disciples to the highest standard: to live according to the righteousness of God himself, for all the world to see. Today, pray that God would enable you to embrace and demonstrate the blessed character that Jesus describes. Ask for strength, by the power of the Holy Spirit, to live as "salt" and "light" in this world for the glory of Jesus. Invite God to continue to shape you more and more into a disciple of Jesus—not only externally, but internally as well!

LESSON 4

THE HEART OF THE LAW

Matthew 5:27–48

THE BIG PICTURE

As we saw in the previous lesson, Jesus began in Matthew 5:21–26 to authoritatively interpret and apply certain commands from the Old Testament law as a demonstration of the fullness of transformation and adherence to God's character that must permeate the lives of his disciples. From murder, Jesus now moves toward adultery, explaining how even hidden lust is a form of adultery and therefore must be battled and defeated (5:27–30). Divorce, except in limited cases, must be rejected, because of Jesus's high view of the value of human marriage and marital fidelity (5:31–32). Jesus then seeks to move his disciples away from an obsession with oaths, insisting rather that they speak truthfully and mean what they say before God (5:33–37). Finally, he again preaches in drastically countercultural fashion by calling his disciples to refrain from taking revenge; rather, they are to actually "love" their enemies and respond with prayer when they are mistreated or abused (5:38–48). He is setting a high bar; in fact, Jesus's call is to nothing less than the perfection of the "heavenly Father" whom his disciples worship and follow (5:48). This, though, is the path of true discipleship, and Jesus's call comes to those who have already become his disciples by God's saving grace. It is a call to holiness—one that begins only when a person submits himself totally to the one who speaks the authoritative Word of God: Jesus himself.

Read Matthew 5:27–48.

GETTING STARTED

1. How have you seen your thought life, imagination, or viewing patterns impact your "real life"—your actions, conversations, or decisions? Discuss how this can be either a positive or a negative reality in the life of a Christian.

2. When you are hurt, wronged, or offended, what tends to be your immediate reaction (before you have time to process, think, and respond)? How does that reaction demonstrate the natural inclination of your heart?

Beyond the External, pg. 151

Jesus told his disciples that they not only must not murder, but must not harbor the anger and contempt that lead to murder. Instead, we should be reconciled to our brothers when something stands between us. . . . Jesus pushed beyond external deeds to probe the motives that lead to murder. Now he does the same thing with adultery.

OBSERVING THE TEXT

3. Consider the categories that Jesus's teaching addresses in this section of Matthew 5. How do these topics—adultery, divorce, promises, retaliation, and behavior toward enemies—cover some of the most basic aspects of life for most people throughout history?

4. What is the common refrain that begins each new section of Jesus's teaching in this passage (5:27, 5:31, etc.)? Why does he use that phrase—and what phrase follows it as his instruction begins? How is this teaching us about the identity of Jesus?

5. How does the chapter conclude? Why is this an intimidating statement/command? If Jesus is not saying that people must be perfect in order to be saved . . . then what is he saying?

UNDERSTANDING THE TEXT

6. How does Jesus show the sin of adultery to be something deeper than the act of adultery itself (5:27–28)? According to Jesus, where does the sin of adultery actually begin, and what can it look like?

7. What guidance does Jesus give for those who struggle with sexual temptation—and how would you describe his tone and approach as he gives it (5:29–30)? How should Christians understand this radical call from Jesus?

8. Why might he have chosen to directly follow this section by teaching on divorce (5:31–32)? What practices had evidently begun in the religious community with regard to divorce? How does Jesus now push back against these practices in defense of marriage?

Careful Speech, pg. 173

So let us hear Jesus' call to truthfulness. Let us measure our words and speak carefully, so that "Yes" means "Yes." Let us describe events without the distortions, theatrics, embellishments, and exaggerations that mislead our neighbors. Let us not claim to know what we do not know. Let us measure each promise so that we mean what we say. Our families, our churches, our society, will be stronger for it.

9. What would you say is Jesus's central point in the section of his teaching about oaths (5:33–37)? What hints do his words contain about oath-taking practices and "rules" that must have been common in Jesus's day? Why is truthfulness such an important characteristic of his followers?

10. How does Jesus call his disciples to respond to those who wrong them, abuse them, or hurt them (5:38–42)? In what ways does Jesus himself practice this teaching at the end of his life?

11. What is so radical about the call to love that Jesus issues at the conclusion of this chapter (5:43–47)? Why does Jesus say that a love for their enemies will so distinguish his followers from the world around them? How does his concluding command, in verse 48, show the ultimate purpose behind all of his teaching and the effect it must have on the lives of those who follow him?

BIBLE CONNECTIONS

12. Read Hosea 2:19–20. How does the marital language that God uses regarding his people teach us about what marriage is meant to represent?

How does this help to explain the seriousness with which Jesus talks about divorce in the passage you have just studied?

13. Read Exodus 21:22–25—one of several places in Old Testament law where the principle of "eye for eye" and "tooth for tooth" serves as a basis for restitution when harm is done. Why might God have included that principle in the law of Moses? How is Jesus saying in Matthew 5:38–42 that this principle must *not* be applied?

THEOLOGY CONNECTIONS

14. John Calvin suggested that God looks at the forgiveness we show our enemies and partly uses it as "a badge by which he excludes from the number of his children all who, prone to revenge and reluctant to forgive, obstinately keep up their enmity, cherishing against others that indignation which they deprecate from themselves" (*Institutes*, 3.20.45). What is Calvin suggesting about the nature of true, Christian forgiveness? How is it evidence of genuine conversion and of the work of the Holy Spirit?

15. The Westminster Shorter Catechism defines sanctification, in the answer to question 35, as "the work of God's free grace, whereby we are renewed in the whole man after the image of God, and are enabled

more and more to die unto sin, and live unto righteousness." How is this a good description and summary of the message of much of Jesus's teaching in this Sermon on the Mount?

APPLYING THE TEXT

16. How have you been guilty of caring more about an outward appearance of holiness and Christian character than about inward holiness and purity? In what ways does this passage call you to repent, confess, and change your heart?

17. In what ways might God be calling you toward a deeper commitment to truthfulness—even when it is painful? What are ways in which you are tempted to subtly deceive others and bend the truth?

The Values of the Kingdom, pg. 185

The values of a disciple are the values of his Lord. The values of the kingdom are the values of the King. We look to Christ. We turn the other cheek because he turned the other cheek. We give generously to all because he gives generously to all. We go the extra mile because he went the extra mile, even with us. For when we . . . were his enemies, he won us with his love.

18. Why is the call to love our enemies such a difficult one? Are there people in your life who have wronged you whom you need to forgive?

PRAYER PROMPT

As you have read and seen throughout this passage, the call to discipleship is a difficult one! The lives of Jesus's disciples are to be modeled after the pattern of their Lord and Savior in terms of purity, truthfulness, faithfulness, integrity, gentleness, and forgiveness. We serve a Savior who intends to transform our internal thoughts and motivations as well as our outward appearances and actions. Today, pray that God would give you a desire for continued growth in purity, honesty, gentleness, and forgiveness of those who hurt you. As a disciple who has already been called to follow him in faith, ask him for grace to pursue this kind of holiness in light of his gracious salvation.

LESSON 5

HOLINESS AND HYPOCRISY

Matthew 6:1–15

THE BIG PICTURE

Throughout Matthew 5, Jesus's teaching focused on the intense moral demands of true discipleship. Men and women who are saved by faith in Jesus are called to the path of righteousness, holiness—and even perfection (5:48)! Not only must their righteousness include outward adherence to the law of God; their thoughts and motives must be transformed by the power and presence of God as well. This is true Christian discipleship; this is sanctification. Now, as we continue through Jesus's sermon by studying Matthew 6, we will see its focus shift toward the way that his followers engage in religious worship, rituals, and obedience. Jesus spoke in the midst of a Jewish culture that maintained rigorous tradition, ritual, and signs of religious piety. But, sadly, those outward actions could all be performed with absolutely no inward change of heart, worship of God, or love of neighbor. Jesus calls us to engage in religious worship and humble obedience—and even a kind of secrecy (6:4). Generous giving is to be done for God's glory rather than for public acclaim (6:1–4). Prayer is to be done with earnest sincerity rather than out of a desire for the admiration of onlookers (6:5–8). Jesus then offers his disciples a model for prayer itself, which includes adoration of God, confession of sin, forgiveness of others, and humble petition. Jesus is offering a picture of religious discipleship that is free from an obsession with outward appearances—and is offered to God, in genuine faith, for his glory alone.

Read Matthew 6:1–15.

GETTING STARTED

1. What are some of the typical signs or indications that someone is a very religious person or a very devout Christian? How are some of those signs and indications quite easy to fake?

2. Why are the motives behind our actions so important? Why might our motives be especially important to God?

OBSERVING THE TEXT

3. Consider the way that Jesus contrasts true religion with the behavior of various religious people of his day ("hypocrites," "Gentiles," and so on) throughout this passage. Based on these contrasts, what do you learn about the way that religion was often practiced in first-century Israel?

Bad Ways to Do Good, pg. 197

We must clarify Jesus' teaching. He does not mean we must always hide our good deeds. He does not say that it is wrong to be seen pray-ing. Rather, it is wrong to pray in order to be seen. He does not say it is wrong to be seen giving a gift to the needy. But it is wrong to give in order to be seen giving.

4. What are some of the motivations that seem to drive people to make demonstrations of religious piety, according to Jesus? How does he identify and label these motivations throughout this passage?

5. What are your initial observations about the model of prayer that Jesus puts before his disciples (6:9–13)? What does he include, and what does he exclude?

UNDERSTANDING THE TEXT

6. How does the motivation behind our religious devotion and activities relate to our ultimate "reward," according to Matthew 6:1–2, 4? What do these verses imply about the audience we should have in mind when we practice righteousness and obedience"?

7. What can we assume about the public fanfare that accompanied almsgiving during Jesus's day, according to Matthew 6:2? How might that look in our context today—and why might it still be subtly tempting for us?

8. Note the contrast between the public prayer and the hidden prayer that Matthew 6:5–6 describes. Is Jesus commanding his disciples never to pray publicly? If not, then what is the main point of this contrast—and of the command that accompanies it regarding prayer?

9. What truths about God does Jesus affirm before instructing his disciples how to pray (6:7–8)? Why are these truths about God fundamental to shaping our attitude and approach to prayer? How do these truths inspire prayers that contrast with the practice of the "Gentiles" whom Jesus mentions?

10. Note the structure of the prayer that Jesus teaches to his disciples (6:9–13). What comes first—and why is this significant? What kinds of petitions are offered? What kind of help does Jesus instruct the disciples to ask from God?

Advantages of Private Prayer, pg. 208
Public prayer is permissible, but genuine prayer finds its voice in private. Public prayer has the distractions of a public situation and the influence of an audience. In private prayer, we can stumble, correct ourselves, and admit that we do not know how to pray.

11. How does Jesus connect forgiveness of others to forgiveness from God (6:14–15)? Why might forgiveness of others be an incredibly important indication of one's grasp of the gospel of Jesus Christ?

BIBLE CONNECTIONS

12. The prophet Amos, among other Old Testament prophets, rails against the religious hypocrisy that so often masks sinful motives and hidden disobedience. Read Amos 5:21–23. How does God react to religious feasts and sacrifices that are performed by people who are living in sin? What warnings should we, as God's people today, take from this prophetic passage?

13. Read Psalm 131—a brief and humble prayer to God. How does this psalm reflect the right attitude of prayer that Jesus teaches in Matthew 6:1–15? How is it evident that the psalmist is not praying for public acclaim or to be noticed by others?

THEOLOGY CONNECTIONS

14. The Westminster Confession of Faith explains the danger of the false assurance that some people feel on the basis of their religious activity and appearance: "Hypocrites, and other unregenerate men, may vainly deceive themselves with false hopes and carnal presumptions of being in the favor of God and estate of salvation" (18.1). How is this sad reality evident in the words of Jesus as he describes the religious climate of his day in Matthew 6:1–15? Where do such "hypocrites" tend to find their assurance and validation?

15. John Calvin explained that the purpose of prayer is not to inform God, beg God, or change God's mind. Rather, Christians pray "in order that they may arouse themselves to seek him."[1] How does the prayer that Jesus teaches his disciples demonstrate this motivation behind praying? In what ways should our prayer shape our hearts and bend our wills toward God's will?

APPLYING THE TEXT

16. How can you better identify sinful motives in your heart that may lie behind "good" deeds or religious activities that you perform? Once

1. John Calvin, *Commentary on a Harmony of the Evangelists: Matthew, Mark, and Luke*, trans. William Pringle (repr., Bellingham, WA: Logos Bible Software, 2010), 1:314.

you identify them, what are steps you can take to confess these false motives and to obey out of a godlier motivation?

17. How might the "Lord's Prayer" shape your own approach to prayer—not through rote repetition of it, but in terms of its general shape, approach, and tone? What lessons should this prayer teach you about the focus you should have as you pray to God?

18. What do you learn in this passage about God's concern for your forgiveness of others? How might you more intentionally and regularly search your heart for any anger or resentment that you are harboring or any forgiveness that you are withholding?

God Forgives the Penitent, pg. 227

Jesus' point is that God forgives the penitent. That is, if we understand how precious it is to be forgiven, if we know how much it cost God to forgive, then we will forgive others. The forgiven have motives to forgive. We thank God for his gift, we admire the beauty of his way, and we hope to do the same for others.

PRAYER PROMPT

Matthew 6:1–15 shines a light on the danger of religious hypocrisy, which is a danger that we all must prayerfully and humbly avoid. Jesus's words warn his disciples against doing the right religious things for the wrong selfish motives—we do not obey, worship, give, or serve for the sake of others' approval but out of joyful worship for our God and Savior. Today, ask that God would search your heart and examine the motives behind your religious service and worship to him. Ask him to enable you to pray with genuine worship, humility, and concern for his acceptance more than for the acceptance of others. Ask him to strengthen you for a religious life that is sincere and free from hypocrisy, so that your outward obedience will spring from your heart's worship of Christ.

LESSON 6

SEEKING HIS KINGDOM FIRST

Matthew 6:16–34

THE BIG PICTURE

As we have already studied, Jesus calls his disciples to religious devotion that comes from the heart, in contrast to religious rituals that are done purely for show. Now, as the Sermon on the Mount continues, Jesus directs his disciples' gaze toward heaven—and toward the eternal values of God's kingdom. Along with prayer and generous giving, as we have already seen, the discipline of fasting is to be done humbly, quietly, and out of worship to God—not for the praise of men (6:16–18). Followers of Jesus find their truest treasure not in money and possessions but in eternal fellowship with God himself (6:19–24). Jesus reserves some of his harshest words of warning for the topic of the dangerous love of money, which can divide one's heart and prohibit worshipful devotion to God alone. Finally, Jesus turns toward the topic of anxiety, which should not capture the hearts and minds of true disciples of God (6:25–34). Disciples of Jesus must reject anxiety and worry, because they know the sovereign and loving care of a good Father, who even cares for birds and flowers! Children of God can rest, without anxiety, in the care of their Savior, as they seek his kingdom above all things and trust his perfect provision.

Read Matthew 6:16–34.

GETTING STARTED

1. In your experience, how do Christians tend to talk about money? What warnings about money have you heard in Christian circles or communities? How have you heard Christians motivate others to show generosity?

2. What are some of the things that people tend to worry about most in your social circle? Which of these things have become somewhat acceptable for people to worry and be anxious about?

OBSERVING THE TEXT

3. Consider Jesus's teachings and warnings about fasting (6:16–18). How are these similar to what he has already taught about prayer and giving to the needy?

Poisonous Posturing, pg. 238

The public display of our works poisons the well. When we fast or give away money and seek credit for it, we do it to impress others and not to seek God. We pretend to act for God, when really we act for ourselves and our audience. We are posers, feigning love for God.

4. What are the specific warnings that Jesus offers his disciples about the love of money and the accumulation of earthly treasure (6:19–24)?

5. How does Jesus effectively use rhetorical questions as he teaches his disciples about anxiety and worry—and about God's care for them (6:25–34)? What is he seeking to remind them about the character of God?

UNDERSTANDING THE TEXT

6. How were some people in Jesus's day abusing the practice of fasting or engaging in it for the wrong reasons (6:16–18)? What, according to Jesus, is the right motivation for and way to practice the discipline of fasting?

7. What are the contrasting "treasures" that Jesus describes in 6:19–21, and what makes them different? How does Jesus's mention of the "eye" of one's body fit into his broader teaching about treasure and money (6:22–23)?

8. Note Jesus's very clear teaching about divided loyalty and service . . . and about the impossibility of serving two masters (6:24). What is the difference between *using* money as a tool and *serving* money in the way that Jesus warns against here?

9. Why does Jesus choose to mention the "birds" and the "lilies" as part of his teaching about anxiety and worry (6:25–31)? What simple lesson that his disciples need to be reminded of is Jesus conveying when he does so? Why is this such an effective teaching tool?

10. How does Matthew 6:33 sum up Jesus's teaching about money, treasure, and anxiety? What does this verse tell Jesus's disciples about their motivation and focus in life? What does it remind us about God's care?

A Dangerous Love, pg. 243

[Jesus'] teaching about money stands in a discussion of discipleship and loyalty to God. Few people set out to live for wealth. No one wants to serve wealth; we want wealth to serve us! Yet the love of money can gradually take control of our hearts. This is the danger, the false god, that Jesus addresses.

11. How does Jesus demonstrate both gentle comfort and stern warning throughout this part of the teaching he gives his disciples? Why are both of these so important for disciples of Jesus?

BIBLE CONNECTIONS

12. Read 1 Timothy 6:6–10. How does Paul's teaching about contentment and money echo Jesus's teaching about money in the passage you have just studied? What does Paul say results from the love of money and from the obsessive pursuit of it?

13. In Luke 12:5–7, Jesus again directs his disciples' attention to the birds and to God's sovereign care over them. What does this passage from Luke suggest that Jesus's disciples *should* worry about, or be concerned about, instead of their daily food and clothing?

THEOLOGY CONNECTIONS

14. John Calvin famously declared the human heart to be an idol factory, referring to sinful humanity's ability to worship and attach ultimate value to almost anything other than the creator God. How can even good things, such as prayer, fasting, and giving, become sources of idolatry when used improperly or out of false motives? What are people worshiping, in such cases, instead of God?

15. The Heidelberg Catechism asks the well-known opening question "What is your only comfort in life and death?" The answer begins, "That I, with body and soul, both in life and death, am not my own, but belong unto my faithful Savior Jesus Christ." How is this answer a good articulation of Jesus's words that are meant to combat his disciples' worry and anxiety (6:25–32)?

APPLYING THE TEXT

16. How might the discipline of fasting be given a good, godly, and appropriate place in your walk with the Lord? What dangers should you avoid as you engage in this discipline? What should your motivation be for doing it?

17. How can you detect the love of money in your heart? What is the difference between carefully saving, spending, and investing money, and being driven by a deep *love* of money? What warning signs might you look for?

18. What tends to cause anxiety and worry in your mind and heart? When you worry, what lies do you tend to believe about God and his character? How can you more intentionally identify sinful anxiety and place your trust in God?

Carefree, pg. 266

Trust in God casts out worry. One can always imagine the future and find a reason to fret. Or we can ponder God's protection of his birds and flowers and find peace. The carefree believer is not reckless. But we are calm as we look at the near horizon, our daily food, and look ahead to the distant horizon, the eternal kingdom.

PRAYER PROMPT

Jesus's teaching in this passage you have just studied calls us away from having an infatuation with the things of this world—whether that infatuation manifests itself in the pursuit of wealth or approval or in constant anxiety and worry. Pray, today, that God would help you by his Spirit to store up treasure in heaven as you walk as a disciple of Jesus. Ask him to guard your heart from worry and anxiety as you rest in his good and sovereign care. Finally, pray for him to graciously convict you of sinful ways in which you fail to value his kingdom above all else.

LESSON 7

BUILDING ON THE ROCK

Matthew 7:1–29

THE BIG PICTURE

Matthew 7 brings us to the conclusion of Jesus's Sermon on the Mount—a sermon in which he has been authoritatively interpreting and applying the law of God for those whom he has called to be his disciples. This path of discipleship is difficult; Jesus calls the gate "narrow" and the way "hard" (7:13–14). But it is the joyful path that those who are saved by faith in Jesus are called to walk—a path that leads to eternal life in the presence of God himself. Matthew 7 begins with a stern warning against the type of judgmental attitude that bypasses one's own sin in order to quickly and haughtily identify the sins of others (7:1–6). Such judgmental hypocrisy leads to one's own judgment before God. Jesus teaches his disciples how to have a proper attitude and approach to prayer, reminding them that their heavenly Father is even more gracious than an earthly father (7:7–11). He warns his disciples about the dangers of religious hypocrisy, reminding them that false teachers can be known by their "fruit" and that on the day of judgment there will be some whose fraudulent religion is publicly exposed (7:15–23). The final picture that Jesus paints for his disciples as he concludes his teaching is one of two houses—each of which has a very different foundation. The house on the "rock," which is built on the words of Jesus, stands firm through storms; the house on the "sand" is destroyed quickly in the midst of trouble (7:24–27). Matthew remarks that the onlooking crowd is amazed by the *authoritative* teaching of Jesus—who, unlike their religious leaders, boldly interprets and applies God's law with regard to himself. He is not only a teacher of the law; he is the Lord and giver of the law.

Read Matthew 7:1–29.

GETTING STARTED

1. In what contexts have you heard people being labeled as "judgmental"? If you have ever been accused of judging someone unfairly, or of having a judgmental attitude, describe what happened. Is there ever a time to "judge" another person?

2. When have you witnessed religious hypocrisy being exposed? Why can that be so devastating and disappointing—especially if the person who is exposed is a Christian leader with significant influence?

> **Bad News and Good News, pg. 279**
> We should begin by asking God to forgive our sins. Jesus' standards are beyond us, but there is good news: Jesus did not come simply to deliver laws; he also came to deliver those who cannot keep his laws. He came to bear the punishment of those who fail to keep his law. He came to teach, but he also came to redeem those who cannot follow his teachings.

OBSERVING THE TEXT

3. Consider the different topics that Jesus covers throughout this chapter. Which ones are familiar, based on earlier themes that we have seen in the Sermon on the Mount? Which are new ideas and concepts that Jesus has not yet taught about?

4. At several points throughout this chapter, Jesus makes statements that seem to summarize the heart of much of his teaching. Identify some of those statements. Explain how they might serve as overarching summaries of some of Jesus's teaching.

5. How does Jesus continue to warn against false religion, hypocrisy, and spiritual fakers throughout this chapter? Why do you think these warnings come up so often in his teaching?

UNDERSTANDING THE TEXT

6. What dangerous tendency do we have with regard to judging others, according to Matthew 7:1–5? Notice that Jesus does not prohibit *all* judgment of others. But what does he call his disciples to do carefully before judging anyone? Why is this often so difficult for us?

7. What kind of attitude does Jesus suggest bringing to prayer in Matthew 7:7–11? How does his illustration involving human fathers teach his disciples about the character and generosity of God the Father?

8. How does Matthew 7:12 capture so much of the heart of the law of God? What do Matthew 7:13–14 admit about the path of discipleship in the footsteps of Jesus? What is implied by the picture of the "narrowness" of the gate?

Asking for Mercy, pg. 290

We simply cannot keep his law. We cannot stop judging others for their failings. We cannot keep even the simplest summary of his teaching: "Do to others what you would have them do to you." What then shall we do? We return to the first word in our passage. We must ask God for mercy to forgive and ask him to make us new.

9. How is Matthew 7:15–23 helpful for shaping our understanding of the possibility of religious hypocrisy and fraud in others? How can we tell if a person is genuinely a follower of Jesus, according to verses 15 through 20? What will be surprising on the day of judgment, according to verses 21 through 23?

10. What is helpful about the imagery of the house on the rock and the house on the sand (7:24–27)? How is Jesus calling his disciples to a deeper understanding of his identity as he calls them to build their lives on his Word?

11. Why are the concluding narrative comments that directly follow the Sermon on the Mount so important to our understanding of the significance of Jesus's teaching (7:28–29)? How is his teaching distinguished from the teaching of the Jewish religious leaders? How do the people respond to Jesus—and what in particular astonishes them?

BIBLE CONNECTIONS

12. In 1 Corinthians 5:9–13, Paul commands the church at Corinth to "judge" unrepentant sinners in their midst; in fact, he is angry that they have not judged these sinners strongly enough! How is this kind of judgment different from the judgmentalism that Jesus warns against in Matthew 7:1–5?

13. Read 2 Peter 2:1–3—the beginning of Peter's description of "false prophets" that plagued the early church in Asia Minor. How do Peter's descriptions match up with the warnings of Jesus in Matthew 7:15–20? In what ways do Jesus and Peter agree regarding the actions and "fruit" of such false teachers?

THEOLOGY CONNECTIONS

14. The answer to question 98 of the Westminster Shorter Catechism defines prayer as "an offering up of our desires unto God for things agreeable to his will, in the name of Christ, with confession of our sins, and thankful acknowledgment of his mercies." How does this definition of prayer agree with Jesus's teaching in Matthew 7:7–11? How does the phrase "things agreeable to his will" help us to understand what we can expect God to give us in response to our prayers?

15. In Matthew 7:22, Jesus describes those who stand before God and claim many good deeds as the reason he should accept them . . . only to be rejected. How might this verse illustrate well the Reformed doctrine of "faith alone"—that it is only faith in Jesus Christ that leads to salvation and acceptance by God?

APPLYING THE TEXT

16. What heart attitude leads you to judge others too quickly? How might you prayerfully and intentionally learn to more quickly and seriously focus on your own sin and weakness rather than on that of others?

17. How should Matthew 7:7–11 shape your approach and attitude when you pray? Should you demand and expect that your every request be immediately granted by God? If not, how can you rightly apply the confidence that Jesus commands when you approach your heavenly Father?

Jesus as Legislator, pg. 310
Jesus challenged the old traditions that the scribes quoted. He was a legislator, not a commentator. He spoke on his own authority, not the authority of others. He insisted on the supremacy of his teaching; the wise build their lives upon his word, for he is the Savior and Lord.

18. What spiritual practices and Christian relationships might help you to detect religious hypocrisy in your heart and life? How can you identify good "fruit" in your life? What role might others in your church community play in helping you to identify sin, hypocrisy, or a lack of good spiritual fruit in your life?

PRAYER PROMPT

Again, Jesus's teaching in Matthew 7 calls us away from mere outward forms of religiosity and toward a deep, genuine, faith-filled path of discipleship in submission to Jesus Christ. Today, as you close your study of this chapter, ask for God to help you to build your life upon the word of Jesus Christ, who died for your sins and enables you to walk a path of discipleship in worship to God. Pray that God would guard you against sinful judgmental attitudes and would enable you to see your own sin more prominently than that of others and to walk humbly in daily repentance. Ask God to make your faith more genuine as you approach him confidently in prayer while trusting in the gracious character of your heavenly Father.

LESSON 8

THE HEALER

Matthew 8:1–34

THE BIG PICTURE

Chapter 8 brings us to a point of transition in Matthew's gospel. For three chapters, we have observed and studied the authoritative teaching of Jesus. It is his word that matters, his word that interprets the law of God, and his word on which all men and women should build the foundation of their lives. As chapter 8 opens, though, we now see Jesus demonstrating the power of his word through powerful signs, or miracles. Jesus is a preacher; we have seen that. But Jesus is also the great Healer who demonstrates the coming of God's kingdom through miraculous signs and wonders that point to his identity as the Messiah and the glorious and comprehensive salvation he brings to God's people. Matthew 8 records accounts of four specific miracles that were performed by Jesus as well as a general summary of many other healings and miracles that he performed in Capernaum as throngs of people flocked to him (8:14–17). Matthew chooses the miracles that he describes very carefully; the ones in this chapter demonstrate Jesus's authority over disease, sickness, the natural world, and even the demonic realm. All things in creation are under the command of the authoritative word of Jesus Christ—so much so that he can even heal from a great distance away through the power of his word (8:5–13). Interestingly, the only section in this chapter that does not record a miracle is a brief interaction between Jesus and an unnamed Jewish scribe and then between Jesus and an unnamed disciple (8:18–22). Perhaps surprisingly, this Jesus who has been performing miracles explains the great cost of following him. The One before whose word all creation trembles will nevertheless walk a path of great suffering—a path that his disciples will walk as well.

Read Matthew 8:1–34.

GETTING STARTED

1. What are some of the skeptical or cynical perspectives that you have heard regarding the Bible's accounts of miracles? Why do some people tend to be skeptical about such accounts?

2. If Jesus had only taught, and had not performed any healings or miracles, what might it be possible to conclude about him? How do miracles play a key role in establishing Jesus's identity as well as his ultimate purpose for God's people?

Savior and Healer, pg. 316

The blind, the deaf, lepers, those who had a flow of blood, and the dead were all unclean. When Jesus touched them, he made them clean. This touch was essential to his ministry. However much we appreciate the teaching of Jesus, we must know that Jesus is more than a teacher. He is the Healer, too. He saves the whole person.

OBSERVING THE TEXT

3. Consider the miracles that Matthew chooses to describe specifically in this chapter, in lieu of many more that he does not recount in detail (see v. 16). Why might have Matthew chosen to record these specific miracles? Pick one or two and explain their particular significance.

4. How would you describe people's responses to Jesus throughout this chapter? How do those whom Jesus heals respond to him? What about his disciples?

5. What aspects of Jesus's identity and purpose are made clear throughout this chapter of Matthew?

UNDERSTANDING THE TEXT

6. What is so significant about the touch of Jesus (8:3)? What is the ironic and surprising result of his touch? Why might Jesus have commanded the leper to say "nothing to anyone" except for the priest (8:4)?

7. What is particularly noteworthy about Jesus's healing of the centurion's servant (8:5–13)? How is this a demonstration of the authority and power of Jesus's word? What is noteworthy about the faith of the centurion, according to Jesus?

8. Why might Matthew have chosen to quote from Old Testament prophecy in 8:17? How does Jesus's fulfillment of this prophecy help us to better understand his identity and ultimate purpose?

Discipleship Comes with a Cost, pg. 339

As people witnessed the mighty deeds of Jesus . . . many concluded that they might wish to become disciples. Seeing this, Jesus had to explain what discipleship entails. He wants no one to underestimate the cost. People may want to follow Jesus on their terms. But just as Jesus wields authority over disease and over nature, so he exercises authority over his disciples. Disciples must follow on his terms.

9. How would you summarize Jesus's responses to the scribe and the disciple (8:18–22)? Why might Matthew have chosen to include this brief interaction in the midst of several accounts of Jesus's miraculous signs and healings?

10. How is the calming of the storm different from the other miracles that Matthew records in this chapter (8:23–27)? What is Jesus proving to his disciples through this miracle? Why is the question in verse 27 so significant—and what is the answer to this question, according to the evidence of this miracle?

11. The final miracle in Matthew 8 shows us an authoritative interaction Jesus has with the powers of the demonic realm. How do the demons demonstrate their acknowledgment of the authority and power of Jesus's word? What is surprising—and sad—about the response of the residents of the area?

BIBLE CONNECTIONS

12. As we have seen, Matthew quotes from Isaiah 53 in the context of Jesus's healing of diseases and sicknesses. Read Isaiah 53:3–6 now, noting the surrounding context of the verse that Matthew quotes. What do you

learn? Why might Matthew be connecting the miracles of Jesus to the "Suffering Servant" song of Isaiah?

13. Skim through Genesis 1, noting its repeated refrain as God creates the heavens and the earth and the seas. In light of this method of creation that God employed, why is it so significant that Jesus "rebuked" the wind and the seas, which led to their immediate obedience to him?

THEOLOGY CONNECTIONS

14. The Westminster Confession of Faith explains that while God typically works through natural and ordinary means, he is "free to work without, above, and against them, at his pleasure" (5.3). How is this a helpful way to understand Jesus's use of miracles during his public and earthly ministry? From what you have studied so far, what would you say were some of his purposes for working in this way?

15. The episode on the boat, when Jesus calms the storm, ought to remind us of the doctrine of the *providence* of God. God's *providence* refers to his perfect and ultimate control over all things—even the storm that shook the boat that held Jesus. How ought this doctrine to comfort you in the midst of difficulty, trials, and suffering?

APPLYING THE TEXT

16. How should Jesus's healing touch of the leper (8:1–4) encourage you today? What can it teach you about your salvation? How does it help you to picture what will happen to God's people when we one day stand in Jesus's presence?

17. Why might some Christians need to be reminded of the cost of following Jesus? How are you tempted to avoid the path of discipleship if it brings suffering or discomfort?

18. Most important to our application of Matthew 8 is the answer to the disciples' question in verse 27: "Who is this?" As you acknowledge Jesus's true identity, what areas of your life do you need to bring into further obedience and submission to him?

The Power of Jesus, pgs. 353–54

[Jesus] leaves the question in the air, "Who is this?" They must ponder it, but we know the rest of the story. We know who Jesus is. He is Lord and Savior. He has power over the storm, but greater still, he has power over sin and death itself. That is why we trust him and follow him.

PRAYER PROMPT

The beautiful heart of Jesus is on full display throughout Matthew 8. He is not just a teacher who lectures from far off. He is the Healer who draws near to offer a healing touch to sick and diseased people in great need. The authoritative word of Jesus both instructs God's people and saves them from their deepest sickness and disease. Today, begin by praising God that Jesus has brought you ultimate, eternal healing. Thank him for the forgiveness of sins, freedom from guilt, and the hope of eternal life. End this study by asking God to give you the courage to count the cost of following Christ and to submit every part of your life to his authoritative word.

LESSON 9

A SAVIOR FOR SINNERS

Matthew 9:1–34

THE BIG PICTURE

As Matthew continues to describe the public ministry of Jesus in chapter 9, it is Jesus's sharp confrontations with the Jewish religious leaders that begin to capture our attention. We have already seen that Jesus is the authoritative Teacher and the great Healer; now we will discover that he is the Savior—and specifically the Savior of *sinners*. Jesus comes for those who are broken, helpless, and in deepest need—rather than for those who are convinced of their own religiosity and self-sufficiency. His first confrontation with the scribes comes in 9:1–8, as his points to his healing of a paralyzed man as evidence that he has the authority to forgive sins. Jesus then calls Matthew, a tax collector, to be his disciple, before gathering to eat with other tax collectors and notorious sinners (9:9–13). This again draws criticism and disapproval from the Pharisees. Jesus explains that his coming is a time of celebration, rather than of mourning, and proceeds to perform his most notable miracle yet: raising a young girl to life from the dead (9:18–26). On the way to do so, Jesus again stops to interact with someone in need, as he brings healing to a woman who has long suffered—and been made unclean—by a discharge of blood. As Jesus continues to heal people—two blind men and a demon-possessed mute man—Matthew describes the shocking response of the religious leaders, who accuse Jesus of getting his power from the devil (9:34). This chapter, then, shows us the heart of this Messiah: he has come for sinners who need him, and his heart is filled with compassion for men and women who are broken. His call to such people, though, is rejected by those whose spiritual pride prohibits them from having compassion or from seeing their own deep need for Jesus.

Read Matthew 9:1–34.

GETTING STARTED

1. What are some ways in which religious pride or hypocrisy can manifest itself? How does a religiously prideful person relate to God? How does such a person relate to people who seem less worthy or upstanding than he or she is?

2. Why are we so prone to forget that the church is meant to be a place that welcomes sinners? How can the church welcome sinners while also pursuing holiness and purity?

The Choice, pg. 375

The Jewish leaders faced a choice between two courses of action, two paths. Would they accept the evidence of Jesus' deity? Would they follow their own reasoning to its conclusion, repent of their skepticism, and believe in Jesus? Tragically, they did not. But their failure instructs us. . . . Unless we believe in Christ, it does no good to know who he is.

OBSERVING THE TEXT

3. Consider the response of the religious leaders to Jesus's healings throughout this passage. How do their responses "bookend" this passage (9:3, 34), and what might Matthew be seeking to explain about these scribes, Pharisees, and teachers of the law?

4. How would you describe the responses to Jesus from the people whom he heals in this passage? How can we learn from—and imitate—their responses to him?

5. What in your initial reading of this passage causes you to grow in your love and admiration for Jesus?

UNDERSTANDING THE TEXT

6. Why might Jesus declare that the paralytic's sins are forgiven before he heals him (9:2)? What is he teaching about his identity and his

authority? How would you describe people's varying responses to Jesus throughout this episode—those of the paralytic, his friends, the scribes, and the crowd (9:1–8)?

7. Why do the Pharisees react so negatively to Jesus's decision to eat with tax collectors and sinners (9:10–11)? What do you notice about Jesus's answer to them (9:12–13)? What is he explaining about his ministry and purpose?

8. What does Jesus seek to explain to his disciples about his coming and his ministry in 9:14–17? Why does fasting not fit with the vibrant public ministry of Jesus?

The Giver of Life, pg. 398

The raising of this girl brings us to a climax of Jesus' mighty deeds. He has healed Jew and Gentile, with a touch and without a touch. He has healed simple diseases, chronic disease, and death. Nothing can resist his power. Jesus is strong, yet tender and generous. . . . He *is* the life-giving stream.

9. How does the account of the raising of the girl and the healing of the bleeding woman further demonstrate the compassionate heart of Jesus (9:18–26)? How might the Jewish religious leaders have responded to a touch from the bleeding woman? What is Jesus demonstrating through his raising of the young girl?

10. What is different, compared to his previous healings, about Jesus's interaction with the two blind men (9:27–29)? What does he seek to discover about them—and why might he do this?

11. The final healing in this passage again demonstrates Jesus's authority over the demonic realm. How do the crowds respond to Jesus (9:33)? What is the devastating and blasphemous response of the Pharisees, and why is it so illogical (9:34)?

BIBLE CONNECTIONS

12. In Matthew 9:13, Jesus quotes a line from the prophet Hosea. Take a few moments to read Hosea 6:1–11. Why might Jesus have chosen

to reference this passage when he was talking to the religious leaders? How and why did the prophet Hosea rebuke God's people?

13. Read 2 Samuel 7:12–16. Why is it so significant that the blind men refer to Jesus as the "Son of David"? What does this phrase reveal about their understanding of the Old Testament—and of Jesus's identity?

THEOLOGY CONNECTIONS

14. Before healing the paralyzed man, Jesus first declares his sins "forgiven" (9:2). Why is this such a massive claim—especially since Jesus has most likely never met this man before? Theologically, what does this claim teach us about our sins—and about the One against whom we ultimately commit every sin?

15. The doctrine of *total depravity* teaches that, while we are not all as bad as we possibly could be, every human being is entirely fallen—every part of their being is affected by sin. We cannot choose God apart from his gracious work in our hearts. How do Jesus's words to the Pharisees in Matthew 9:12–13 point to the truth of this doctrine? What do we need to acknowledge in order to truly come to God in faith and repentance?

APPLYING THE TEXT

16. How might you be guilty of classifying some people as being "out of reach" of God's grace? How can this passage call you to make a compassionate commitment to pray for lost sinners and to point them to Jesus?

17. What can this passage show you about your need for Jesus—and about your helpless state apart from him? How can what you have studied today make you more grateful for the salvation, healing, and forgiveness you have received?

18. How can you imitate the heart and actions that Jesus displays in today's passage?

So We Might See and Believe, pg. 410

Jesus is the healer. With ease, he gives light to the eyes. If he delays, it is only so we can follow the sign, so we see and believe that Jesus gives light to the eyes and to the heart. He is the light of the world, strong enough to heal, tender enough to take all the time we need, so we can finish with him.

PRAYER PROMPT

Jesus, the great Teacher and Healer, has come for sinners. What good news this is! Jesus demonstrates his compassion as he opens blind eyes, heals paralyzed legs, casts out demons, and allows unclean people to draw near and touch him. Today, count yourself as one of the needy and helpless sinners who joyfully draw near to Jesus in order to be made well. Ask God to show you your sin, your need, and your weakness so that you might find your strength and healing in his Son. Then pray that God would give you a heart like Jesus's so that you may invite sinners to follow him and to know his healing grace as well.

LESSON 10

THE MISSION

Matthew 9:35–10:42

THE BIG PICTURE

As we have seen, Jesus's ministry on earth has been *multifaceted* and complex; he is the authoritative Teacher but also the compassionate Healer. Up to this point, Jesus's disciples have been mainly observers—have been watching in awe as he teaches, heals, casts out demons, and even raises people from the dead. Now, though, Jesus begins to teach his disciples about their part in his ministry—about the mission to which he has called them. Our passage today begins with Jesus urging his disciples to pray for more laborers for the harvest, as he looks with compassion on a world in great need (9:36–38). Then Jesus calls the twelve disciples to himself, as Matthew names each of them for the first time (10:1–4). To these men Jesus gives a mission: he sends them to preach about the kingdom of God, cast out demons, and heal the sick—all through his authoritative power (10:5–15). This mission, he warns, will not be easy. They should expect suffering, persecution, and even death; the servants of Jesus will often receive the same brutal treatment and rejection that their master did (10:24–25). Even so, the disciples of Jesus can go into the world on their mission for him without fear, knowing that they will one day stand before the God they have proclaimed and served (10:26–33). The message they proclaim will bring division, persecution, and even hatred (10:34–39), but service and obedience to Jesus will bring an eternal reward (10:40–42). While we as Christians today are different from these twelve disciples of Jesus, this passage still ought to significantly shape our understanding of our mission in this fallen world. We proclaim Jesus as Savior and Lord, expecting that proclamation to bring suffering and resistance but placing our hope in the eternal reward we will receive in the presence of our God.

Read Matthew 9:35–10:42.

GETTING STARTED

1. What is exciting about being sent on a special mission or endeavor? How or when have you experienced the excitement of that kind of commissioning?

2. Why can it be such a temptation for some Christians to withdraw from the world and settle for a private, quiet, and even secretive faith in Jesus?

A Mission to Fulfill, pg. 411

Like a great player who then becomes a coach, Jesus trains others in his skill. . . . In Matthew 10, the work of Jesus expands. He begins to train and commission his team. He prepares them to take his message, his power, and his cause to the world. He tells them—and us—to fulfill the mission God gives in the way Jesus shows.

OBSERVING THE TEXT

3. How do Matthew 9:37–38 serve as theme verses for this passage you are studying? What is Jesus communicating to his disciples about their role in his mission to the world?

4. What is exciting about the mission that Jesus presents to his disciples? What is potentially frightening and intimidating about it? What can we learn from this?

5. In what ways does Jesus point to eternal rewards for his disciples' service to him and his mission, even as he honestly presents the suffering and difficulty that accompany this service?

UNDERSTANDING THE TEXT

6. What do you observe about the men whom Jesus calls to be his disciples (10:1–4)? What does Matthew seem to want you to notice about them? How does Jesus immediately equip and empower them?

7. What specific instructions does Jesus give to his disciples as he sends them out on their mission (10:5–15)? How does he predict the different responses they will receive—and how are they to react to these different responses?

8. How does Jesus prepare his disciples for persecution, rejection, and suffering (10:16–25)? What will equip and prepare them for difficult moments of trial and witness? What should encourage them, in the midst of this suffering, with regard to their connection to Jesus?

9. How do Jesus's words in 10:26–33 point his disciples to an eternal perspective on their mission, their suffering, and their reward? In what way should the future vision of God's acceptance of them motivate them in the midst of their earthly mission—and in the face of the earthly rejection they will face?

God Will Deliver, pg. 444

To be Jesus' disciple and messenger is to court persecution. But fear not, Scripture says. If we suffer, we follow the path of Christ, who suffered and then entered glory. Fear not, for if God cares for sparrows and hairs, he certainly cares for us when we suffer. Fear no man, Jesus says, but do fear God who can deliver or condemn. In the end, he will deliver you.

10. What further divisions, disagreements, and difficulties does Jesus predict for his disciples when they truly follow him (10:34–39)? What encouragement and promise does Jesus include in these verses for those who sacrifice greatly for him?

11. How does 10:40–42 bring a fitting conclusion to this section of the gospel of Matthew? What blessings does it promise to those who support the mission of Jesus and who accept those who minister in his name?

BIBLE CONNECTIONS

12. In Ezekiel 34:2–5, God condemns the leaders of his people for their abuse of the people and for their failure to shepherd them faithfully and gently. Read those verses now. How might the theme of those verses from Ezekiel inform Jesus's perspective as he looks out at the helpless crowd at the beginning of this passage (Matt. 9:36–38)?

13. Read 2 Corinthians 11:23–28, in which Paul describes the suffering he has experienced as an apostle of the Lord Jesus Christ. How do Paul's suffering and persecution in the midst of his mission fulfill Jesus's words

and warnings to his disciples in this passage? How can we learn from, and be encouraged by, the apostle Paul in his suffering?

THEOLOGY CONNECTIONS

14. The answer to question 28 of the Heidelberg Catechism offers these encouraging words about the providence of God: "We may be patient in adversity, thankful in prosperity, and with a view to the future may have good confidence in our faithful God and Father that no creature shall separate us from His love." How does this statement echo the encouraging words of Jesus in Matthew 10:26–33? How can these truths strengthen us against the fear of man?

15. John Calvin, in his *Institutes of the Christian Religion*, remarks that "we are superstitiously timid, I say, if whenever creatures threaten us or forcibly terrorize us we become as fearful as if they had some intrinsic power to harm us" (1.16.3). How does this statement relate to Jesus's words in Matthew 10:28? What must we remember about the power of this world in relation to the eternal power of our God—and how must that impact what we truly fear?

APPLYING THE TEXT

16. How should Jesus's commissioning and sending of his disciples encourage and inspire you as his disciple today? Why is it surprising and wonderful that he entrusts his gospel, ministry, and kingdom work to those who follow him?

17. What causes you to shrink back from wholeheartedly serving Jesus in the areas of your bold witness to the gospel, deeds of mercy, and support of other ministers of Christ? How might this passage be calling you toward a deeper engagement with Christ's mission in the world?

18. How can we, as followers of Jesus, more lovingly and generously "receive" those who serve the name and cause of Jesus (10:40)? What might this look like—both for you individually and for your church community?

The Weight of the Smallest Deed, pg. 455

Even the smallest deed, done in Jesus' name, has weight. The smallest deed links with God's cause, the cause supreme. It advances his kingdom and transports us into partnership with the apostles, the prophets, and Jesus himself. A small deed is great because it joins God's great project of restoring all things. A small deed reaps a great reward because it enters into the work of the kingdom and of Christ.

PRAYER PROMPT

Jesus's public earthly ministry was strikingly brief, lasting only three years. But his commission to his disciples (which is developed more finally at the conclusion of Matthew's gospel) reminds us that Jesus's mission and ministry continue through his people. Today, ask God for strength to boldly and sacrificially take up the cause of Jesus Christ and his kingdom. Pray for courage to proclaim the gospel of Christ, even when doing so brings rejection, social marginalization, or shame. Ask God for an eternal perspective—to help you to remember the eternal reward that is yours through faith in Jesus Christ!

LESSON 11

DOUBT, OPPOSITION, AND FAITH

Matthew 11:1–12:21

THE BIG PICTURE

As Matthew 11 opens, we are confronted with some doubts about Jesus from an unlikely person: John the Baptist. Even this great prophetic forerunner of Jesus seems to struggle with the trajectory of Jesus's ministry and the suffering that it brings—John asks, from prison, whether Jesus is the Messiah or whether God's people should wait for someone else (11:3). Jesus responds with words of comfort and assurance for John before moving on to a wider discussion of his reception in the world (11:16–24). People reject him for various reasons; but no matter their reason for doing so, judgment will come on people and places who do not accept Jesus as the Son of God (v. 24). Those who do accept Jesus, though, receive eternal rest for their souls (11:25–30).

The first two accounts in Matthew 12 take us to the battleground of the Sabbath, as Jesus allows his disciples to pluck grain, and also heals a man with a withered hand, on the Sabbath day (12:1–14). The Pharisees, who are obsessed with the legality of Sabbath regulations, respond to Jesus with angry condemnation. In light of this intense opposition, Jesus withdraws and continues his ministry in a more secretive fashion (12:15–21). Matthew summarizes the ministry of Jesus through the prophetic words of Isaiah, who looked ahead to a gentle Servant who would lift up the needy and bring God's love and grace to even the Gentile peoples of the world.

Read Matthew 11:1–12:21.

GETTING STARTED

1. If you have struggled with doubt in the past—about God, the Bible, or your own faith—what factors seemed to give rise to that doubt? How did you deal with it? What strengthened your confidence in God, his Word, and the reality of your relationship with Christ?

2. Why might legalism be such a common and pernicious problem in religious circles? What is appealing about legalism? Why can it do such damage to gospel faith and community?

Willing to Bend, pgs. 460–61

Jesus blesses those who are teachable, who are willing to bend their thoughts to his. John nearly stumbled over his preconceived ideas about the Savior. Both John and the Pharisees were startled by the form of Jesus' ministry, when it seemed that he might be the Redeemer. The difference between them is that John changed his opinion of his opinions, whereas the Pharisees did not.

OBSERVING THE TEXT

3. What factors might have led to John the Baptist's question to Jesus? Why is it important for us to understand that even this prophet struggled with doubt about Jesus's identity, mission, and purpose?

4. What are some of the negative reactions to Jesus that we see throughout this passage? What seems to be motivating Jesus's opponents when they object so strongly to what he is doing?

5. As you read through this passage, what do you find to be most appealing about the ministry and character of Jesus? How is he contrasted with the religious leaders of his day? What do you notice about his words of invitation and about his treatment of people in need?

UNDERSTANDING THE TEXT

6. How would you summarize Jesus's answer to John the Baptist's doubtful question (11:4–6)? What does Jesus point to in order to make his identity, purpose, and mission clear for John the Baptist and his disciples?

What does Jesus say about John the Baptist—and how does he explain the role that he played in Jesus's life and ministry (11:7–11)?

7. What has been the general response to the prophets—and to Jesus himself—according to his words in 11:16–24? How does Jesus accuse the people of being difficult to please? Why will judgment be so severe for those in Jesus's day who reject his teaching and invitation (vv. 20–24)?

8. How does Jesus describe the dealings that God the Father has with different kinds of people (11:25–26)? How about the relationship that he has to God the Son (11:27)? Why is this relational unity and the purpose behind these dealings so important for us to understand? What do you find encouraging about Jesus's invitation in 11:28–30? What does this tell you about his heart for his people?

David and his companions ate the shewbread in the tabernacle. No one was to eat except the priests. They didn't understand the Word.

9. Why do the Pharisees object to Jesus's disciples plucking heads of grain on the Sabbath (12:1–2)? How does Jesus use the Old Testament in his response to them? What point does he make about the ultimate purpose of the Sabbath day?

Pharisees have rigid rules. Jesus teaches 2 important lessons- He is Lord of the Sabbath- He designs it as a day of worship + service. He teaches us about His identity and character. It is a good day for acts of kindness.

10. What additional truth about the ultimate purpose of the Sabbath does Jesus introduce through his healing of the man with the withered hand (12:9–12)? What is so devastating about the response of the Pharisees—and what does it reveal about their hearts (12:14)?

11. How is Jesus's ministry fulfilling Isaiah's prophetic words about God's chosen Servant (12:18–21)? What do you notice about this particular prophecy, with regard to the people whom God's Servant will gather and rule over?

The Essence of the Law, pg. 495

If we capture the true intent of the law, it always leads us to love God and love our neighbor. Any interpretation of the law that limits our ability to serve God or to love our neighbors—as the Bible, including the Decalogue, defines love—must be wrong, because love of God and love of neighbor are the essence of the law (Matt. 22:34–40). No particular law can ever forbid the essence of the Sabbath—loving God.

BIBLE CONNECTIONS

12. Malachi 3:1 tells of the "messenger" who will come before the Messiah. Read that verse now. What is the significance of Jesus's connecting this prophetic word to the ministry of John the Baptist?

13. Read 1 Samuel 21:1–10—the account of David that is referenced by Jesus in Matthew 12:3–4. What was David's purpose behind eating the consecrated bread—and why did the priest allow him to have it? Explain the argument Jesus was making by referencing this account in relation to his disciples eating heads of grain.

THEOLOGY CONNECTIONS

14. The Westminster Confession of Faith explains the purpose of the Sabbath day in this way: "This Sabbath is then kept holy unto the Lord, when men, after a due preparing of their hearts, and ordering of their common affairs beforehand, do not only observe an holy rest, all the day, from their own works, words, and thoughts about their worldly employments and recreations, but also are taken up, the whole time, in the public and private exercises of his worship, and in the duties of necessity and mercy" (21.8). How is this explanation of the purpose of the Sabbath consistent with Jesus's teaching in the passage you have just studied?

15. The doctrine of the Trinity is central to orthodox Christian teaching. What important teaching about the Trinity does Matthew 11:25–27 contain? What does it teach about the deity of both the Father and the Son, as well as about their distinction as persons of the Godhead?

APPLYING THE TEXT

16. How can you intentionally, honestly, and biblically deal with doubt when it comes? What role should the people of God who are in your church play in your struggle with doubt?

17. What warnings ought you to hear—and heed—from this passage regarding legalism? How can the Pharisees serve as a negative example of putting rules before people, regulations before healing, and legalism before God himself?

The Great Healer, pg. 511

Above all, [Jesus] is gentle. Instead of quarreling with the Pharisees, he withdraws. More important, he is gentle with us. Yes, he bruises us, but only to show us our need of him. Bruises move us from our self-made religions to true faith. The Pharisees remind us that man-made religion is the foe of true faith in Christ. Jesus is the great healer.

18. How should Jesus's invitation in Matthew 11:28–30 shape your understanding of his call to you? While discipleship in service of Jesus is not easy, what do these verses remind us about his heart for his people?

PRAYER PROMPT

Throughout this passage you have just studied, you have seen various responses that people have to Jesus. The great prophet, John the Baptist, struggles with doubts. The nameless crowds are never satisfied by Jesus, just as God's people in years past had ultimately rejected the prophets. The Pharisees allow their legalistic impulses to crowd out the true meaning of the Sabbath. Jesus, though, is the gentle Savior who invites people from all nations to submit to his gracious rule. Today, pray that God would gently remove your doubts and grant you grace to submit to the rule of Jesus in every area of your life. Ask him to give you the grace to share his gentle heart for those who are in need of his love and salvation.

LESSON 12

FOR HIM OR AGAINST HIM

Matthew 12:22–50

THE BIG PICTURE

You have already seen, in your study of Matthew, the increased intensity of the opposition to Jesus—particularly on the part of the religious leaders and authorities. Now, in the passage for this lesson, the hostility, tension, and hatred toward Jesus only increases. The Pharisees accuse him of casting out demons through the power of Satan, leading to Jesus's harsh condemnation of this blasphemy against the Holy Spirit (12:22–32). Jesus goes on to condemn the bad "fruit" that emerges from hard and sinful hearts, warning the Pharisees that their evil words against him will bear witness against *them* on the day of judgment (12:33–37). When the Pharisees disingenuously ask Jesus for a "sign," he again detects their hypocrisy and points them to the sign of Jonah—even the Ninevites repented, because of Jonah's preaching, which is yet another indictment against the hard hearts of the Pharisees (12:38–42). The passage ends with yet another startling word of warning—but also with a word of comfort. As Jesus's own mother and brothers seek to speak to him (perhaps to convince him to stop, or slow down, his public ministry), he refuses to go with them (12:46–50). The true family of Jesus consists of those who do the will of the "Father"—not those who are related to him biologically through Mary (v. 50). So, even as we see the increasing hardening of Jesus's opponents throughout this passage, we find a warm invitation that is available to all: Jesus invites all people to accept him as Messiah, obey the will of God the Father, and become part of his spiritual family.

Read Matthew 12:22–50.

GETTING STARTED

1. We often think, "If I had lived in Jesus's day, I would never have rejected him like the Pharisees and Jewish teachers of the law did!" Based on what you have read and studied so far, what did these religious leaders find so threatening about Jesus? How might we have to admit that we have some similarities with them, when we see the parts of our own lives or religious practices that Jesus threatens?

2. What have you heard being taught in Christian circles about the "unforgivable sin"—a concept derived primarily from this passage in Matthew? Have you ever been frightened, or concerned, about committing this sin—this "blasphemy" against the Holy Spirit? Explain.

Different Standards, pg. 513

To the Pharisees and teachers, Jesus looked like one of them in many ways. He taught the law and gathered disciples to himself. So it offended them when he did not follow their standards. In other words, if Jesus were simply a lawless man, the leaders would have ignored him. They watched Jesus because, from the beginning, he looked like a religious leader. But he did not behave the way they thought a leader should.

OBSERVING THE TEXT

3. Note the tone of Jesus's words to the Pharisees in this passage. How is he confronting their words and behavior? How would you describe the way that he speaks to them, along with the force of his words?

4. What role does Satan (and his demonic realm) play in this passage? How is Jesus demonstrating his authority over evil spiritual forces?

5. What do you notice about the conclusion of the passage? What is surprising about Jesus's response to his earthly family? How might this episode relate to his previous interactions with the Pharisees?

UNDERSTANDING THE TEXT

6. How do the Pharisees misattribute the power of Jesus (12:24)? What might they be seeking to accomplish? How does Jesus respond to their accusation, and what impresses you about his response?

7. Matthew 12:31–32 are difficult and disputed verses. Given their context, what does Jesus mean by "blasphemy" against the Holy Spirit? Why ought we to see this "unforgivable sin" as something that is done only intentionally, willfully, and unmistakably?

8. How are we to recognize true believers in Jesus, according to Matthew 12:33–37? What is so important about the Pharisees' words—and our own words (vv. 36–37)?

9. What is ironic about the demand of the Pharisees in 12:38? What signs have they already seen from Jesus in the parts of Matthew you have studied so far? What can you conclude about the motivation behind and sincerity of their question to Jesus, and how does this shed light on the way in which Jesus responds to their request (12:39–42)?

Never Enough, pg. 528

We see, therefore, how Israel's leaders could surround Jesus and ask for another sign. Given that they just saw a sign from God and ascribed it to the devil, they have considerable nerve. They had seen or heard other reports that Jesus had healed lepers, the paralyzed, the blind, and the lame. . . . Jesus had offered plenty of signs, but they were never enough.

10. What might Jesus be teaching through his illustration of a heart that is temporarily "swept clean" of demonic possession (12:43–45)? How does this story demonstrate our need for total heart transformation and change? In what ways have the Pharisees revealed that they lack that kind of change?

11. How does Jesus teach about the true family of God in Matthew 12:46–50? What is frightening about these verses? What is deeply encouraging about them?

BIBLE CONNECTIONS

12. When the Pharisees asked Jesus for a sign, he pointed them back to the reluctant Old Testament prophet, Jonah. Interestingly, Jonah performed no signs; but he did ultimately preach to unbelieving Gentiles who repented and turned in faith to God. Why might Jesus have chosen to point the Pharisees to the "sign" of Jonah? What is he seeking to teach them about their responsibility before God?

13. Read 1 Kings 10:1–13—the episode that is referenced by Jesus in Matthew 12:42. How did the Queen of Sheba respond to the wisdom and blessing of King Solomon and his kingdom? How *should* her response have been a model for the way in which the Pharisees responded to Jesus Christ, the greater King?

THEOLOGY CONNECTIONS

14. The Westminster Confession of Faith asserts that "as there is no sin so small but it deserves damnation; so there is no sin so great that it can bring damnation upon those who truly repent" (15.4). What does this statement remind us about God's grace to even the greatest sinners? Is any sin "unforgivable" if a person truly repents and places his or her faith in Jesus?

15. In the Reformed tradition, we talk often of the beauty of the *adoption* that we have as we are brought into the family of God by faith in Jesus. How does Matthew 12:46–50 beautifully illustrate this doctrine of adoption?

APPLYING THE TEXT

16. What do your words reveal about you? How can you commit to having more accountability with regard to your speech, in light of Jesus's words in Matthew 12:34–37?

17. Given Jesus's words of warning to the Pharisees about their responsibility on the day of judgment, how ought this passage to wake us up to our responsibility with regard to Jesus today? What is the right response to God, given all that we now know about his Word, his Son, and his gospel?

18. How should Jesus's words about his true "mother and brothers" encourage you if you are truly doing the will of God by following, trusting, and loving Jesus (12:50)? How can your understanding of your spiritual "family" strengthen your faith?

Listen and Believe, pg. 530

We have not seen Jesus with our eyes or heard him with our ears, yet we have heard the message of Jesus from reliable witnesses. We too know far more than the people of Nineveh, more than the Queen of the South, more even than those who heard Jesus preach. Therefore we are responsible to listen and to believe or else to face the consequences.

PRAYER PROMPT

Even after countless signs and miracles, the Pharisees still refused to place their faith in Jesus—even going so far as to accuse him of working with Satan to cast out demons! Today, ask God for the grace to enable you to keep placing your faith in Jesus with joy, humility, and obedience. Praise him that he counts you as part of his true family when you do his will. Finally, ask him for strength to boldly bear witness to him—to invite others to repent and join the family of God.

LESSON 13

PARABLES

Matthew 13:1-58

THE BIG PICTURE

We have seen Jesus teach before; we spent several lessons exploring his extended, authoritative explanation and application of God's law in Matthew 5–7. Now we study another collection of Jesus's teachings—ones that are somewhat different. Matthew 13 records several of Jesus's *parables* for us, which he taught in the presence of throngs of people who were crowded around him (13:1–2). These stories are lessons about the kingdom of God, the gospel, and the coming of Jesus, which are disguised and veiled in significant ways. This is intentional on Jesus's part; he explains that the veiled nature of his teaching is in fulfillment of the Old Testament prophets, who wrote of the blindness and deafness that people have apart from God's saving work (13:11–17). To his disciples, though, Jesus takes time to clearly and carefully explain his parables so that they can understand (13:18–23; 36–43). Through these parables, he teaches about the different responses people have to the Word of God that he proclaims, about the eternal value of the kingdom of God, and about the patience of God as both unbelievers and believers dwell together and await the final judgment of the world. His disciples learn of the immense treasure of the kingdom of God, which is attained through faith in Jesus Christ. Sadly, not all understand . . . and some from Jesus's own hometown reject him and his message completely (13:53–58). As we have seen before, Jesus and his gospel will be eternal life for some—but will be rejected by others.

Read Matthew 13:1–58.

GETTING STARTED

1. Why do stories and illustrations help to make a lesson more understandable and memorable? Can you think of examples of this from a recent lecture, sermon, or small-group discussion?

2. What do you love about the parables of Jesus? How can they be challenging or confusing? What are some principles for interpreting and applying Jesus's parables that you have found helpful in the past?

The Secrets of the Kingdom, pg. 549

Jesus speaks in parables because of a sovereign decision. He reveals the secrets of the kingdom as he wills (13:11). When Jesus speaks in parables, "whoever has" receives more, while "whoever does not have" loses what he has (13:12). The one who "has" is the person who already knows the person and the work of Jesus and wants to know more. The one who "does not have" has seen the same events, but neither cares nor believes.

OBSERVING THE TEXT

3. What is different about this chapter's teaching compared to the previous teachings of Jesus that you have studied? Note the setting, the audience, and the style of the teaching in this chapter, in contrast with previous passages you have studied.

4. How does Jesus make use of illustrations and stories that would have been familiar to his audience? To whom does he explain his parables, and why?

5. What is surprising about the way that this chapter concludes—with Jesus's rejection in his hometown of Nazareth? Why might Jesus's own friends and relatives have been the most skeptical about his identity and ministry?

UNDERSTANDING THE TEXT

6. What do you notice about the audience for Jesus's teaching as this chapter begins (13:1–2)? How is this different from the primary audience for

his teaching in Matthew 5–7? As Jesus tells this first parable (13:3–9), what might have been difficult for people to understand?

7. What does Jesus explain about the purpose of his parables (Matthew 13:10–17)? What is surprising to you about his explanation—and perhaps contrary to what we might expect? How does this help you to understand the mystery of the gospel as well as people's need for the Holy Spirit to enable them to truly believe?

8. How would you summarize the main point of the parable of the sower, according to Jesus's explanation of it in 13:18–23? Why would this parable have been important to Jesus's disciples as they prepared to preach the good news of the gospel of Jesus Christ?

God Knows His People, pg. 569

The parable of the wheat and the weeds adds a new thought. While the righteous and the wicked grow together, they can be indistinguishable for a time. It may be impossible to tell believers from unbelievers, but God knows his people. Eventually, he will separate the righteous and the wicked. He will judge and remove the wicked, but will reward the righteous and bring them into his presence.

9. What seems to be the main emphasis of the parable of the weeds (13: 24–30)? How does Jesus explain the meaning of this parable (13:36–43)? Why is the parable meant to be both encouraging and frightening for the people of God?

10. What truths about the kingdom of God is Jesus explaining in the briefer parables of 13:44–52? What do we learn about the *value* of the kingdom of God? What do we learn about its hidden nature? What surprises you about what Jesus teaches regarding God's kingdom?

11. What response does Jesus receive from those in his hometown of Nazareth (13:53–58)? How does he respond in turn? Why might he have chosen to respond this way?

BIBLE CONNECTIONS

12. The longest Old Testament quotation in this chapter comes from Isaiah 6; take a moment now to read Isaiah 6:1–10. Why might Jesus have chosen to quote from this passage as he explained his use of parables?

What do you notice about the immediate context of those words in Isaiah 6, and how might that context relate to the ministry of Jesus?

13. Read 2 Thessalonians 1:5–10, and note what it teaches about the final separation on the day of judgment. How does this passage from the apostle Paul agree with Jesus's teachings about the day of judgment in the passage you have just studied (Matt. 13:41–42, 49–50)?

THEOLOGY CONNECTIONS

14. The doctrine of regeneration teaches that because of human sinfulness and spiritual blindness, the Holy Spirit must revive us, illuminate our minds, and miraculously regenerate our hearts for faith in Jesus Christ. How do the blindness and the deafness that Jesus describes in Matthew 13:13 explain our need for regeneration? In what ways do Jesus's parables illustrate this doctrine as well?

15. The term "the invisible church" is a way of speaking about all genuine believers throughout history. The "visible church," according to the Westminster Confession of Faith, consists of "all those throughout the world that profess the true religion, together with their children:

and is the kingdom of the Lord Jesus Christ, the house and family of God, out of which there is no ordinary possibility of salvation" (25.2). How is this doctrine of the visible and invisible church taught in Jesus's parable of the weeds?

APPLYING THE TEXT

16. What can Jesus's parable of the sower teach you about your own proclamation of the gospel—and about the different responses you can expect to receive? How should this parable motivate you to have a bolder and more courageous gospel witness?

17. How should the parable of the weeds cause you to think about the community of the church? How can you guard against cynicism and suspicion while also expecting genuine fruit from fellow believers in Jesus Christ?

Our Great Treasure, pg. 589
The kingdom grows slowly, but it is God's supreme gift and our great treasure. Jesus' concluding remark certainly summons us to hear, believe, and treasure the gospel of the kingdom.

18. How is this passage calling you to more fully treasure the kingdom of Jesus? How might God be calling you to invest more radically in his kingdom—the "pearl" of greatest price?

PRAYER PROMPT

Even though Jesus's teaching is hidden to some, God opens the eyes of his true disciples to understand the wisdom of the kingdom that Jesus reveals. Today, if you believe in Jesus, thank God that he has opened your eyes, unstopped your ears, and softened your heart to receive the life-giving gospel. That is his gift—not something you have earned! Pray for boldness to proclaim the gospel of the kingdom. Pray for faithfulness to press on in obedience to Jesus. And ask God to help you to value his kingdom above all things—to help you even to be willing to sacrifice worldly treasure, honor, and glory in order to finally receive it.

Jon Nielson is senior pastor of Spring Valley Presbyterian Church in Roselle, Illinois, and the author of *Bible Study: A Student's Guide,* among other books. He has served in pastoral positions at Holy Trinity Church, Chicago, and College Church, Wheaton, Illinois, and as director of training for the Charles Simeon Trust.

Daniel M. Doriani (PhD, Westminster Theological Seminary; STM, Yale Divinity School) is professor of theology and vice president at Covenant Theological Seminary. He is the founder and president of The Center for Faith and Work in St. Louis and a member of the Council of The Gospel Coalition.

P&R PUBLISHING'S COMPANION COMMENTARY

Daniel Doriani, a pastor and scholar recognized for his works on biblical interpretation, furnishes readers with Christ-centered commentary and personal and corporate applications. Each chapter of this two-volume work seeks to express Matthew's original intent in ways that evoke his distinct voice and thereby fulfill the goal of his gospel—making disciples by forming the mind, heart, and hands of believers.

The Reformed Expository Commentary (REC) series is accessible to both pastors and lay readers. Each volume in the series provides exposition that gives careful attention to the biblical text, is doctrinally Reformed, focuses on Christ through the lens of redemptive history, and applies the Bible to our contemporary setting.

Praise for the Reformed Expository Commentary Series

"Well-researched and well-reasoned, practical and pastoral, shrewd, solid, and searching." —**J. I. Packer**

"A rare combination of biblical insight, theological substance, and pastoral application." —**Al Mohler**

"Here, rigorous expository methodology, nuanced biblical theology, and pastoral passion combine." —**R. Kent Hughes**